Leading Curriculum Improvement

Fundamentals for School Principals

Marilyn Tallerico

ROWMAN & LITTLEFIELD EDUCATION
A division of
ROWMAN & LITTLEFIELD PUBLISHERS, INC.
Lanham • New York • Toronto • Plymouth, UK

Published by Rowman & Littlefield Education
A division of Rowman & Littlefield Publishers, Inc.
A wholly owned subsidiary of The Rowman & Littlefield Publishing Group, Inc.
4501 Forbes Boulevard, Suite 200, Lanham, Maryland 20706
http://www.rowmaneducation.com

Estover Road, Plymouth PL6 7PY, United Kingdom

British Library Cataloguing in Publication Information Available

Library of Congress Cataloging-in-Publication Data
Tallerico, Marilyn.
    Leading curriculum improvement : fundamentals for school principals /
Marilyn Tallerico.
        p. cm.
    Includes bibliographical references and index.
    ISBN 978-1-61048-408-4 (cloth : alk. paper) — ISBN 978-1-61048-409-1
    (pbk. : alk. paper) — ISBN 978-1-61048-410-7 (electronic : alk. paper)
    1. Curriculum change. 2. School improvement programs. 3. Educational leadership.
I. Title.
LB1570.T215 2012
375.006—dc23   2011035359

Printed in the United States of America

~

Contents

~

Preface

Today's school administrators need to capitalize on multiple pathways for increasing student learning. Improved curricula are one such avenue. And this book offers clear guidance for facilitating curriculum improvement effectively.

Although most states or districts prescribe standards and assessments—and some provide curriculum frameworks—much work remains to be done at the building level. Why? Because:

- Neighborhood demographics can vary widely from one school to another, often necessitating specialized programming.
- Teachers' talents and school cultures are unique, each requiring close-at-hand leadership support in order to thrive.
- Curriculum implementation in classrooms can look quite different from what may be envisioned by distant policy-makers.
- Strong curricula do not magically spring forth from long lists of subject standards, instructional manuals, or assessment results.

For all of these reasons, informed leadership and continuous local curriculum improvement are important responsibilities for principals. The ideas, examples, and strategies shared in this book will help school leaders execute those responsibilities well.

How Is the Book Organized, and Why?

The book is structured around seven "essential questions" that capture key concepts in curriculum leadership. This approach *models* for readers what contemporary experts routinely recommend as means of focusing curriculum priorities and increasing relevance for learners. That is, it is built around a limited number of "big ideas."

Each chapter begins with a short, attention-grabbing vignette illustrative of real-life scenarios encountered by school leaders. From that vignette, additional subquestions engage the reader while introducing and forecasting the chapter's substance.

The book's working title is aimed at capturing its substantive scope: that is, *fundamentals* for busy educators looking to update or refresh their understandings of curriculum leadership. It is a guidebook, rather than an encyclopedia of everything known about the topic. It provides enough background to interest and inform target audiences, without overwhelming them with theory and details. In short, it is a selective overview of curriculum improvement fundamentals, organized around the questions:

- Which big ideas set the stage for curriculum leadership?
- How can leaders help focus the curriculum?
- When is curriculum mapping useful?
- What are other curriculum support strategies?
- Where do more integrated models come in?
- What about alternatives to standardized curricula? and
- Why do philosophy and political leadership matter?

This scope may be better understood in contrast to that of other authors. That is, whole volumes are often dedicated to particular curriculum improvement approaches (for example, aligning taught and tested curricula, designing curricula backward, or mapping the curriculum). Similarly, many books focus on single subject areas (e.g., improving literacy, teaching mathematics well, or writing across the curriculum).

However, principals and other school leaders are, for the most part, generalists. Their time for reading is limited. Yet they are eager to stay current, and to hone their knowledge and skills. These professional realities drive the book's content, structure, tone, and scope. Hence, it centers on actionable ideas and approaches that can be applied across multiple school subjects and grade levels. It succinctly illustrates a range of field-tested practices for leading curriculum improvement. It cogently synthesizes guiding concepts and strategies selected for their potential usefulness to practitioners.

Simultaneously, its grounding in the work of renowned experts and its up-to-date references provide ample additional resources for readers who wish to pursue topics in greater depth or detail.

For Whom Is This Book Written and How Might It Be Used?

The short answer is that target audiences are: (1) current and aspiring K–12 principals, and (2) educational leadership professors.

The longer response is that this book focuses on contemporary issues and strategies useful to practicing professionals. The term "principal" is used as shorthand. The actionable ideas emphasized are equally applicable to the work of assistant principals, teacher leaders, instructional coordinators, and others responsible for curriculum improvement in K–12 schools.

At the same time, the book will appeal to those college professors who prepare prospective administrators of all sorts because the concepts and examples highlighted are rooted in the work of renowned scholars and professional experts. It is a serious yet accessible book, providing thoughtful syntheses of best practices and research-based implications for both current and future educational leaders.

How might it be used? This book is aimed at helping its primary audience lead (that is, plan, facilitate, support, coordinate, and oversee) continuous curriculum improvement in schools. It does that by: (a) increasing readers' understanding of relevant knowledge-bases, (b) linking that knowledge to the real world of today's schools, (c) providing practical examples and strategies, and (d) connecting curriculum leadership to student learning. By reading this book, current and prospective school leaders will be better equipped to decide among varied curriculum improvement approaches, design and implement those options well, and build constituencies' support for improvement initiatives. They will also learn how integrated curricula and other alternatives to standardized programming can complement standards-driven foci.

What Other Benefits Does This Book Offer?

As alluded to earlier, notable features are:

- The book's selectivity and scope,
- The timeliness and importance of its content, and
- Its organization around essential questions relevant to school leaders.

Additional benefits are that the book:

- Concisely synthesizes research, key concepts, and expert insights on best practices in curriculum improvement and leadership
- Integrates ideas drawn from varied professional literatures, including those important to curriculum design, principal leadership, adult learning, school improvement, and change facilitation
- Translates this knowledge base into implications and suggested steps that building leaders can take to guide and enhance their school's curriculum. These practical strategies are both big-picture and doable. They are rooted in inclusive, collaborative approaches that engage and facilitate teachers' work
- Connects principals' curriculum improvement efforts to student learning, consistently underscoring the *educational* in educational leadership

What, More Specifically, Will You Find in This Book?

Chapter 1 introduces ideas fundamental to understanding the big picture of a school's intended, supported, unwritten, experienced, and learned curriculum. It illustrates why such distinctions matter, how key concepts relate to one another, and where principals' leadership comes in. This chapter sets the stage for all that follows in the book. It does so by connecting curriculum improvement to principals' roles in setting direction, developing staff, and enhancing school conditions to promote student learning.

To flesh out the theme of learning-centered leadership, *chapter 2* offers strategies for helping teachers cut through the clutter of state and district standards, to sharpen the school curriculum's focus. Examples include how to collaboratively develop curriculum priorities, pacing guides, common assessments, and curriculum units centered on essential questions. All of these strategies involve groups of teachers working together toward important goals. To help principals support and sustain that work, chapter 2 reviews best practices for sharing leadership, facilitating productive meetings, and keeping collective efforts focused on agreed-upon curriculum improvement directions.

Chapter 3 centers on curriculum mapping, another leadership tool for coordinating the educational program and increasing coherence for students. This chapter describes and illustrates the various phases involved in mapping effectively. It addresses what school principals can do to facilitate these processes. Emphasis is on mapping's usefulness for systematically fine-tuning the scope and sequencing of curriculum subject areas across multiple teachers and grade levels. Besides clarifying the benefits of mapping and suggesting ways principals can help, chapter 3 also surfaces several caveats.

The next chapter introduces additional curriculum support strategies, to supplement those elaborated in chapters 2 and 3. *Chapter 4* begins with guidelines for managing recurring curriculum operations. Examples include clear and teacher-friendly systems for sharing information, managing data, and acquiring or adopting instructional materials. These essential though largely maintenance-oriented administrative supports are then contrasted with change-oriented curriculum leadership. To facilitate the latter, chapter 4 offers key questions to guide the creation of new curricula. The chapter concludes by summarizing recent research on effective professional development, to inform principals' efforts to help staff continuously improve.

Chapter 5 addresses issues of curriculum fragmentation, imbalances, and disconnects that can develop over time. The chapter explains and illustrates how student learning can be enhanced by teaching usually separated school subjects together; that is, through a more integrated curriculum. Examples of four different possibilities for integration are distinguished, including fusion, multidisciplinary, interdisciplinary, and transdisciplinary approaches. Additionally, a half-dozen strategies are offered for how school principals can facilitate and sustain integrated curricula. Examples include critically analyzing integrative themes and paving the way with school publics.

The ensuing chapter extends several of the ideas introduced as integrated approaches, to explore additional alternatives to commonplace curriculum and school improvement practices. *Chapter 6* challenges educational leaders to guard against excessive curriculum standardization, while addressing the needs of students who may be unsuccessful in conventionally organized programs. The chapter provides four extended examples of what such alternatives can look and sound like: two at secondary schools, and two at the elementary level. Each incorporates distinctive strategies for personalizing and increasing the relevance of curricula.

Chapter 7 builds on both the standards-based emphases of chapters 2–4 and the less conventional curriculum alternatives of chapters 5 and 6. It does so by tackling the question, What kind of education do we want for our children? This chapter illuminates the diverse ideological and political environments in which U.S. schools operate. It underscores the value of school leaders' self-awareness, empathy, and informed policy influence. Chapter 7 also offers tools principals can use to communicate shared goals, map political contexts, reconcile differences, and build coalitions supportive of curriculum improvement directions.

A final chapter wraps up and reinforces several of the book's most salient themes. It is followed by a carefully selected reference list, to enable readers to pursue in greater depth and detail any of the information or strategies synthesized in this volume.

~

Acknowledgments

I am indebted to the researchers, practitioners, theorists, and professional associations whose studies, insights, and perspectives helped inform this work. Heartfelt appreciation is also extended to Chris Ritter for his unwavering personal support and encouragement. I am grateful to Binghamton University and School of Education Dean S.G. Grant for making possible the sabbatical leave that facilitated this project. Additionally, I wish to thank the acquisitions, editorial, and production teams at Rowman & Littlefield Education, whose skills and assistance were essential to this volume. Special thanks also go to the following individuals whose feedback, suggestions, and thoughtful critiques helped shape initial drafts of this book:

Louise Cleveland
    Education Consultant
    Transforming Learning Communities
    Susquehanna, Pennsylvania
Abe Feuerstein
    Associate Dean of Faculty
    College of Arts and Sciences
    Bucknell University
    Lewisburg, Pennsylvania
Sandra Lee Gupton
    Professor of Educational Leadership
    University of North Florida
    Jacksonville, Florida

Ruth G. King
 NAESP 2010 National Distinguished Principal
 Homer Elementary School
 Homer, New York
Sanford E. Nelson
 NAESP 2010 National Distinguished Principal
 Rossman Elementary School
 Detroit Lakes, Minnesota
Kristin Sherwood
 Principal
 Derby High School
 Derby, Kansas

And lastly, I greatly appreciate the reprint permissions granted by Eye On Education and ASCD, as follows:

Selection: Figure 2.1. Pacing Guide (Curriculum Component)
 Adapted from Rettig, M. et al. (2004), *From rigorous standards to student achievement: A practical process.* Larchmont, NY: Eye On Education, p. 12.
Selection: 1-Page Template with Questions
 Source: From *Understanding by design: Professional development workbook* (p. 30) by Grant Wiggins & Jay McTighe, Alexandria, VA: ASCD. © 2004 by ASCD. Reprinted and adapted with permission. Learn more about ASCD at www.ascd.org.
Selection: Sample Curriculum Map: First Draft
 Source: From *Getting results with curriculum mapping* (p. 87, Fig. 7.2), by Heidi Hayes Jacobs (Ed.), Alexandria, VA: ASCD. © 2004 by ASCD. Reprinted with permission. Learn more about ASCD at www.ascd.org.
Selection: Interdisciplinary Concept Model
 Source: From *Interdisciplinary curriculum: Design and implementation* (p. 57, Fig. 5.2 "Interdisciplinary concept model: A Unit on Flight – Steps 1 and 2"), by Heidi Hayes Jacobs (Ed.), Alexandria, VA: ASCD. © 1989 by ASCD. Reprinted with permission. Learn more about ASCD at www.ascd.org.

1

~

Which Big Ideas Set the Stage for Curriculum Leadership?

The principal calls a school secretary into his office and asks, "What's this phone message from the new school board member about?" The secretary fills him in: "She wants to shadow a couple of students so she can learn about the social studies curriculum." He thinks to himself, "Well she could learn a lot more about it if she spent an hour with the department chair and read the social studies curriculum guide our teachers spent weeks revising just last summer."

What helps explain how differently this school board member and principal are thinking about the curriculum? How do student, teacher, and community understandings of educational programs interrelate? Why are school-based curriculum leaders essential?

Research linking leadership and student learning drives some of the answers to these important questions. So too do several key conceptual distinctions. Together, these foundational understandings set the stage for facilitating curriculum improvements.

Why School Curriculum Is Important

Everyone wants good schools. Yet school quality is characterized by innumerable variables: students' learning and well-being, teachers' competence and continuing development, leadership and resources, parental engagement and community support, physical facilities and educational climate. The list goes on and on, depending upon values and worldviews.

1

At its core, however, the *substance* of a school is its educational program (English, 2010; Leithwood & Montgomery, 1986; Wiles, 2009). In shorthand terms, that program is commonly referred to as the curriculum. Although more nuanced distinctions will be discussed later, in its simplest form, a curriculum may be thought of as *content*, a synonym for substance. That content includes the ideas, knowledge, skills, and dispositions that schools seek to cultivate among students. This substantive core may be structured as constellations of required and elective courses at the secondary level. It is reflected in continua of subjects addressed throughout the elementary grades. And it encompasses the specialized programming for students at any level, including enrichment, remediation, athletics, and other activities or supports.

Understanding curriculum as substance accentuates its centrality to the work of teachers and administrators, and its significance to public perception of particular schools. Moreover, the curriculum's coherence, rigor, and relevance shape schools' most valued outcome—what students learn (Glatthorn & Jailall, 2009; Parkay, Hass, & Anctil, 2010). For all of these reasons, a school's educational program is important.

Where Administrative Leadership Comes In

Strong school and district leadership creates and sustains the conditions, processes, structures, and policies that serve this substance well. For example, recent research finds that principals influence student learning in three main ways: by setting direction, by developing people, and by making the school organization work (Leithwood, Louis, Anderson, & Wahlstrom, 2004; Murphy, Elliott, Goldring, & Porter, 2006; Wahlstrom, Seashore Louis, Leithwood, & Anderson, 2010). Although ensuing chapters provide additional examples of what each of these three responsibilities looks and sounds like in practice, let's start with an overview.

Applied to leading curriculum improvement, *direction-setting* involves:

- *Collaboratively establishing priorities.* What will our curricula emphasize, include, and leave out? Addressing these questions recognizes that the substantive knowledge-base is vast and dynamic, and that each school community is unique. Consequently, thoughtful decisions must be made to determine where foci should be (Reeves, 2006).
- *Keeping collective efforts focused on those priorities.* Is it a priority if the school's attention shifts from one program emphasis to another each year? Perseverance, time, and support are required to enable any change initiative to

take hold and flourish (Fullan, 2007). Through their big-picture vantage points, communication about what's important, and oversight functions, principals can help sustain curriculum improvements over time.

Complementing principals' roles in collective direction-setting, *developing people* means:

- *Supporting teachers' and staff's on-the-job learning.* The knowledge-base keeps expanding, research on best practices continuously evolves, and new technologies emerge every week. Accordingly, school and district leaders need to sustain opportunities for ongoing adult learning, particularly around teaching specific academic content (Darling-Hammond et al., 2009; Garet, Porter, Desimone, Birman, & York, 2001; Tallerico, 2005).
- *Facilitating collaboration and teamwork.* Just as program priorities need to be decided upon collectively, so too must leadership be shared for curriculum development, implementation, and assessment work. This means involving and capitalizing on broad ranges of teachers', specialized staff, and community expertise (Allen, 2007; Spillane, 2006). It also means developing teamwork and collaboration skills as part of professional learning opportunities.

Making the organization work for program improvement involves both administrative management and leadership roles for principals, including:

- *Ensuring that school structures support the curriculum.* Smoothly functioning systems need to be created and maintained for essential operations (Wiles, 2009). Basics include teacher-friendly arrangements for acquiring instructional materials and supplies, for sharing facilities, and for updating technologies. Beyond the basics is making sure that district policies complement one another so that, together, they bolster rather than undermine curriculum priorities.
- *Fostering positive climate and culture.* Principals serve as role models for where a school's attention is focused (Murphy et al., 2006). They are also tone-setters for the kinds of relationships and communications most valued (Sergiovanni, 2006). Hence, how much time principals devote to the instructional program, the ways in which they share leadership, and their success in building parents' understanding and community support for curriculum priorities are all part of enhancing the organizational conditions that make schools work well.

Throughout the book, we revisit and expand upon these three overarching ways in which principals influence student learning. At this time, however, several key concepts also warrant introduction. These ideas and vocabulary comprise essential understandings for leading curriculum improvement. They also move us beyond our preliminary focus on curriculum as content, to refine and deepen the meaning of curriculum leadership.

Perennial Debate

Expert opinion varies on what "curriculum" actually means. For example, Glickman, Gordon, and Ross-Gordon (2009) define the term as "the moral deliberation on what is 'right' for students to be taught" (p. 281). They elaborate by explaining that the range of possible learning emphases is great, that narrowing that range involves thoughtful, collaborative decision-making, that reasonable people hold differing visions of what a "good" education encompasses, and that "most teachers—when trusted, when given time and money, and when given the assistance, choice, and responsibility to develop curricula—will make extraordinarily sound decisions about what students should be taught" (p. 283).

To illustrate a contrasting expert perspective, Hass (1987) defines curriculum as "the set of actual experiences and perceptions of the experiences that each individual learner has of his or her program of education" (p. 2). Like the first, this definition of curriculum acknowledges that there is a formal program of studies that is purposefully organized and presented in school. However, this characterization is more student- than teaching-centered, emphasizing instead what children learn and how they feel about their experience in school.

We could continue teasing apart the scores of curriculum definitions that have appeared in the professional literature over time. We would likely find that the variance among them reflects differing emphases and combinations of what have classically been referred to as the four "commonplaces" of curriculum:

- Subject matter
- Teacher
- Learner
- Milieu (a term we'd probably replace today with either context or environment)

While debate about the relative influence and connections among these four main variables persists, busy building leaders may find other sets of distinctions more useful. Therefore, we turn our attention next to the written and unwritten curriculum, as well as the taught, tested, supported, experienced, and learned curricula.

Helpful Distinctions and Implications for Principals

The definitions that follow draw primarily from the summaries of others (English, 2010; Glatthorn, Boschee, & Whitehead, 2006). Here, we supplement those syntheses with original graphic organizers and elaboration particular to principals' work.

In the contemporary, standards-based environment of U.S. schools, educators' time and effort are frequently concentrated on the *intended* curriculum, illustrated by the triangle in figure 1.1.

The Written Curriculum

The written curriculum takes many forms. Examples include state standards for what students should know and be able to do in different subject areas; professional organizations' content recommendations (e.g., the National Council of Teachers of Mathematics' standards); district-developed documents with titles such as "English Language Arts curriculum guide," "PreK–12 Social Studies curriculum map," or "Scope and sequence for science instruction"; course syllabi at secondary grade levels; specialized program handbooks (e.g., for the International Baccalaureate or Reading First programs); teachers' manuals provided by textbook publishers; and teacher-developed lesson plans.

Written curricula often communicate the ideals and aims of individuals or groups of teachers, administrators, and other experts concerned with

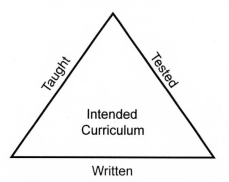

Figure 1.1. The Intended Curriculum.

what ought to be taught and learned in schools. Their intended audience is typically teachers and sometimes parents and community members. The purposes of such documents range from guiding and coordinating instruction, to organizing and prescribing the taught curriculum, to informing key constituencies.

The Taught Curriculum

The taught curriculum is the curriculum in practice, as translated, personalized, and enacted by teachers in individual classrooms. Some define the taught curriculum as "the delivered curriculum, a curriculum that an observer would see in action as the teacher taught" (Glatthorn et al., 2006, p. 14). Distinguishing the taught from the written helps to appreciate curriculum as more than a selected body of content knowledge or standards. Content must also be communicated and engaged with learners in particular settings (Au, 2007). Hence, the taught curriculum blurs the lines between substance and pedagogy; between *what* is intended and *how* it is taught (Segall, 2004). Curriculum and instruction are inextricably intertwined.

Given the current context of accountability via standards-based assessment, the taught curriculum may also be thought of as a subset of the written curriculum. That is, principals can likely trust that most teachers work purposefully to incorporate and address the written, consensus expectations and standards for their grade level, subject areas, and programs. Additionally, because written curricula typically include more aspirations and intended content than can be engaged in actual classrooms, teaching necessarily involves individual decision-making, interpretation, and ad hoc adaptation for particular students—even when the written document is one's own lesson plan.

It is essential, therefore, that school leaders recognize both the limitedness of the written curriculum, and the complexities of the taught curriculum. It is also important to remember that the taught curriculum is more directly connected to students' *experience* of the educational program than the written.

Although such reminders may seem unnecessary, we encourage school and district leaders to consider how much time and attention are devoted to creating and refining written documents (e.g., curriculum maps, frameworks, guidebooks, etc.), compared to the resources dedicated to supporting the taught curriculum. Of course, it is difficult to quantify the professional learning benefits that can be derived from the collective deliberation, analysis, and reflection that go into developing written curricula collaboratively. Nonetheless, mindfulness about the distinction between written and taught curricula is vital.

The Tested Curriculum

The tested curriculum is what is assessed; that is, those parts of the curriculum that students are evaluated on. Like written and taught curricula, tested curricula vary widely. Variations may be partially due to an assessment's intended purpose. For example, one purpose is diagnostic (e.g., How can we tell which students need additional help with math facts? Which computation skills warrant reteaching?). Another possible purpose is formative (e.g., How can information about the strengths and weaknesses of students' oral reports help them improve their presentations next time?). Other purposes are summative and attached to significant consequences, hence the term "high-stakes" tests (e.g., Who will be promoted to the next grade? Which students have displayed sufficient grasp of the freshman English curriculum to pass to sophomore English? Who will graduate, or not?).

Beyond purpose, other variations in tested curriculum relate to the assessment's development. For example, many quizzes and exams are teacher-made for single classrooms or district-developed for particular grade-level subjects and courses. Although such assessments may have the advantage of being closest to the taught curriculum and to particular groups of students, teachers and local collaborators vary greatly in their ability to create sound evaluations. By comparison, testing companies and textbook publishers typically have greater assessment-development expertise, as well as resources to pilot assessments, enhance test validity and reliability, and build robust banks of test items. However, this know-how comes at a cost, both financial and in terms of increased distance from local school contexts.

What are some implications for school leaders? Clearly, in today's environment of high-stakes assessment, the tested curriculum matters. Therefore, some amount of coordinated effort must be dedicated to ensuring that the taught and tested curricula are congruent. Congruence, in this context, means that students are afforded ample opportunities to learn what they will be evaluated on, and teachers are supported in their work to craft such opportunities. (Congruence as curriculum "alignment" will be elaborated in chapter 3.)

At the same time, principals may also need to be champions of taught curriculum *breadth* and tested curriculum *balance*. The latter means continuing to allocate resources to diagnostic, formative, and multiple means of student assessment, even though pressure to focus exclusively on high-stakes summative testing may be intense (Abrams & Madaus, 2003).

Similarly, championing taught curriculum breadth involves advocacy for a well-rounded set of learning experiences, including those aimed at children's social, emotional, artistic, and physical development. Such advocacy is needed to counter forces that, at minimum, disproportionately skew resources toward state-tested subjects and, at worst, push schools to become testing factories (Spring, 2005). Recent studies confirm that high-stakes testing narrows the taught curriculum to tested subjects, "to the detriment or exclusion of nontested subjects" (Au, 2007, p. 263). Often, the arts, second languages, and elementary-level social studies are the losers as emphases on reading, writing, math, and science increase (Von Zastrow & Jance, 2004).

The Supported Curriculum
The supported curriculum is also a part of the intended curriculum, although not depicted graphically in figure 1.1. As one might guess from the label, supports connote resources; in this case, resources to back, bolster, and reinforce the written, taught, or tested curriculum. Because advocacy for, acquisition, and allocation of resources are leadership responsibilities, principals feature prominently in the curriculum that gets supported at the building level. Examples include:

- Scheduling and time allocations (e.g., Will all grades have uninterrupted reading time or just primary classrooms? Which subjects or teachers might be advantaged or disadvantaged by the master schedule?)
- Student assignment and staffing decisions (e.g., How will low-achieving students be distributed among fourth-grade teachers? Which classrooms will have instructional aides? What will class size be for inclusive classrooms?)
- Professional development (e.g., Are our top learning priorities the same as those of other schools in the district? If not, where will we focus, and who can assist with our building's needs? With whom will literacy coaches spend most of their day?)
- Books, other instructional materials, technology, and supplies (e.g., In which classrooms will SmartBoards be installed in year 1 allocations? What special materials and accommodations are warranted for the high proportion of English language learners in our school?)

Principals' knowledge of curriculum and instruction, along with interpersonal and communication skills, can go a long way to bolster the taught curriculum, teaching, and learning *within* their schools (Marzano, Waters, & McNulty, 2005). Moreover, building leaders' creativity, reasoning, assertiveness, and political savvy shapes the distribution of district resources *to* individual schools (Fowler, 2004).

In addition to these overt manifestations of the supported curriculum, principals' tone-setting, modeling, and culture-building also influence the norms and unspoken taken-for-granteds of particular schools. For this reason, it is equally important to understand the concept of the implicit curriculum. (See circle in figure 1.2.)

The Unwritten Curriculum

The unwritten curriculum is part of what is learned and lived by students in schools, although it is neither planned nor intentionally taught. As illustrated in figure 1.2, the unwritten curriculum is a significant aspect of every school; a filter through which written, taught, and tested curricula are experienced and viewed by students.

Synonyms include the implicit and the informal curriculum. "Hidden" curriculum is the phrase perhaps most frequently used; however it can imply deliberate concealment (Blumberg & Blumberg, 1994) and, therefore, is inconsistent with our meaning here.

We use the adjective unwritten because it succinctly captures the contrast with what were previously introduced as intended curricula: written,

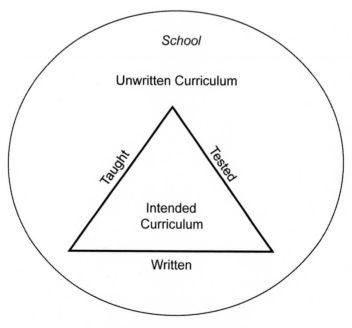

Figure 1.2. School Curricula.

taught, and tested. Additionally, "unwritten" seems to us a less value-laden term that can help steer clear of the common misconception that the hidden curriculum is exclusively negative or undesirable.

For example, on the one hand, some students may observe, experience, and internalize that:

- Athletes sometimes receive lighter disciplinary consequences than other students; therefore, which social group you mix with matters.
- Most teachers like conforming and compliant students better than those who question assignments or rules; so, lay low and you'll likely pass.
- White and nonwhite students sit in different parts of the cafeteria; therefore, segregated socializing is normal.

On the other hand, children may also see, live, and learn that:

- Students feel respected and valued at this school; therefore, you can anticipate being treated fairly and well.
- Most teachers go out of their way to assist struggling pupils; so, it's okay to admit that you don't understand or need extra help.
- Nonwhite and white students routinely study and play together here; therefore, integration is normal.

These examples illustrate a range of positive and negative messages that stay with students, even though not explicitly taught or voiced. Studies of what graduates remember and value most about their education point to the powerful and long-lasting influence of such unspoken messages (Blumberg & Blumberg, 1994; Little, 2001; Wolk, 2008). This unwritten curriculum includes the feel, norms, and values implicit in classrooms and schools.

What's this have to do with building leadership? Because of the unwritten curriculum's power, it is important that principals work to understand the meanings students make of school structures, practices, and climate. Becoming familiar with the unwritten curriculum's "takeaways" for students can shed light on how the school's culture complements or undermines its intended curriculum. Facilitating conversations about what memories teachers would want their students to carry through a lifetime could sharpen the focus of collective efforts for school improvement.

Perhaps ironically, raising implicit school messages to the level of collective consciousness for examination and purposeful change blurs the boundaries between the unwritten and intended curricula. That is, the unwritten then becomes part of the planned curriculum. In the leadership literature, such efforts to change the school environment for the better are commonly referred to as *culture-building* or *reculturing* (Fullan, 2007). We revisit and elaborate principals' roles in tone-setting and nurturing positive school culture in subsequent chapters.

Sociopolitical Context

Of course, sociopolitical context also shapes the intended and unwritten curricula. As illustrated by the large oval in figure 1.3, each school is part of a broader social and political environment.

Some obvious sources of influence on the intended school curriculum include:

- *Educational governance structures.* For example, currently, each state prescribes content standards for most subject areas. The federal No Child Left Behind Act of 2001 requires annual student testing in English language arts and math in grades 3–8. Local school boards often approve teacher hiring and authorize district-specific curricula or assessments.
- *Federal, state, and local politics.* Might the 50 states come to consensus on national standards for what students should know and be able to do? Will your district receive increased, decreased, or static funding for its educational program over the next several years? Could a community group mobilize around the dropout rate published in the local newspaper, ushering in pressures for particular curriculum directions?
- *Opportunities and supports.* For example, a regional educational unit incentivizes certain professional development, curriculum enhancement, or student assessment services. Since they are less expensive and handier than going it alone, your district opts in, perhaps simultaneously supporting yet reshaping your school's collective priorities or attention. Grant monies, local foundation initiatives, and neighboring universities' programs or research interests can have similar impacts.

Other more amorphous sources of influence on the unwritten curriculum include:

- *Ideology and social values.* What are prevalent societal beliefs and biases about racial, social class, sexual orientation, ability, or ethnic diversity? How do those beliefs and biases manifest in the unstated yet widely understood status of different students or groups in schools? What might children be learning when they see that most U.S. senators and governors are male and most elementary teachers are female?

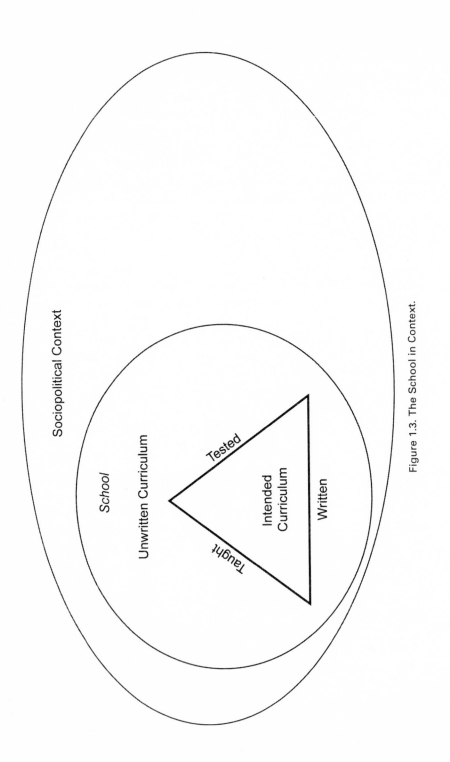

Figure 1.3. The School in Context.

- *Youth culture.* Outside of school, children and youth are increasingly engaged with technologies and media of various kinds. Inside, they may need to hide their cell phones or help teachers exploit their computers' potential. What might some students take away from mismatches between how they communicate and learn for fun and what they experience in school?

Taken together, these social and political influences provide parameters—both constraints and opportunities—within which local curricula are designed and brought to life. Typically, these parameters leave considerable room for school-level creativity, adaptation, and responsiveness to particular students' needs and communities' interests. However, strong leadership is required to foster and guide that creativity, adaptation, and responsiveness toward shared goals for children's learning and well-being (Marzano et al., 2005; Murphy et al., 2006; Wahlstrom et al., 2010).

Importantly, the principal is the public face of the individual school to the constituencies that comprise this broader sociopolitical context. Principals also serve mediating, boundary-spanning, and buffering roles because of their position at the intersection of external and internal school constituencies. We elaborate these roles, and strategies for making the most of social and political opportunities, later in the book.

The Experienced Curriculum
The experienced curriculum refers to the vantage points of students: how learners perceive and "live" what is intended and implicit in schooling. In figure 1.4, the experienced curriculum is depicted as a rectangle that spans the written, taught, tested, and unwritten curricula. Its overlap with the triangular and circled concepts is partial because we seldom know how much of—or how—the intended and unwritten curricula are actually experienced by students.

The rectangle extends into the sociopolitical context, to suggest how integral students' out-of-school lives are to their educational experiences. Similarly, strong curriculum leadership builds bridges that blur the boundaries between schools and their communities (Allen, 2007). Questions for curriculum teams to consider include: How do students feel about how their families or home cultures are treated in school? Which school programs capitalize on community resources and opportunities that students might perceive as part of their "real" worlds? How can school and regional social services be connected to create more integrated experiences for children?

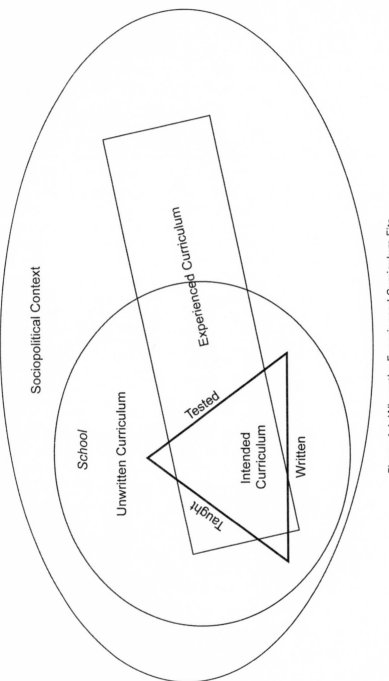

Figure 1.4. Where the Experienced Curriculum Fits.

The Learned Curriculum

The learned curriculum is what students take away, understand, internalize, and retain from all other curricula. It involves individual students' interpretations, sense-making, and reconstruction of knowledge and experience. It "denotes all the changes in values, perceptions, and behavior that occur as a result of school experiences" (Glatthorn et al., 2006, p. 15).

The learned curriculum is not illustrated in any of our graphics, although how and where to represent it in figure 1.4 would be a useful question for a school faculty to grapple with. Perhaps it may be understood as either a subset, or an extension, of the experienced curriculum.

Clearly, what is learned is a product of many interacting variables (e.g., the student, the instruction, the substance of programs, access to educational opportunities), some of which the school has little or no control over (e.g., societal trends, children's home lives or health). Nonetheless, student learning should be central to curriculum and leadership work—the pivotal outcome toward which our collective energies are aimed. As analyses of educational leadership research and theory remind us, learning-centered leaders are results-driven, knowledgeable about, and deeply involved in the school's curricular and instructional programs (Marzano et al., 2005; Murphy et al., 2006).

A Final Thought

A recurrent message throughout this overview of key concepts is that both leadership and curriculum are means to an end. That end—our shared purpose and main goal—is student learning and well-being. Although not the *only* means to these desired outcomes, leadership and curriculum are pivotal contributors, often setting apart outstanding schools from average ones.

To flesh out the themes of learning-centered leadership (Murphy et al., 2006) and starting with the end in mind (Covey, 1989), we turn next to strategies for cutting through the clutter and advancing curriculum priorities.

2

~

How Can Leaders Help
Focus the Curriculum?

Principals in neighboring districts have added new character education programs in their schools and enthusiastically recommend you do too. Your superintendent returns from the annual conference of the American Association for School Administrators, where she saw a dynamic presentation on service learning. She asks you to pull together a group of teachers to explore project-based learning through community service. At the same time, the regional educational center is promoting a countywide math curriculum development initiative and requests your school's participation.

How can principals enhance learning for students without signing on for every new opportunity that presents itself? On what should teacher teams be spending their scarce collaboration time? What strategies can leaders use to focus, rather than continually expand, the school's intended and experienced curricula?

Three points for school leaders to keep in mind as they address these and other questions are:

- There is truth to the cliché, "Less is more."
- Priority-setting requires leadership.
- Curriculum improvement takes sustained collaboration.

Why Focus Is Important

There is no shortage of public calls for higher standards for schools. But higher has often morphed into *more*: more school services, more specialized programs, more required testing, and more academic curriculum targets.

This chapter is about prioritizing *fewer* content standards for the taught and tested curricula at the school level. Why? State standards tend to consist of overly ambitious listings for each subject. Moreover, textbooks are frequently "a mile wide and an inch deep" (McTighe, Seif, & Wiggins, 2004). Together, these written curricula can leave teachers and students overwhelmed or idiosyncratically presuming what is essential to know and be able to do (Newmann, 2010).

As introduced in the previous chapter, direction-setting is one of three main ways that principals influence student learning (Leithwood, Louis, Anderson, & Wahlstrom, 2004; Wahlstrom, Seashore Louis, Leithwood, & Anderson, 2010). Direction-setting here means collaboratively establishing priorities for *which* standards a school curriculum will emphasize, include, or leave out. It involves cutting through the clutter. In this chapter, we explain several ways leaders can help focus what is realistically teachable and, more importantly, what can bring about deeper understanding by students.

Streamline Curriculum Content Standards

One process for prioritizing state standards involves reflection, deliberation, and collaborative decision-making centered on three questions. (Unless otherwise cited, the information in this section is derived from Reeves, 2006.) See box 2.1.

- **Which standards capture knowledge or skills that *facilitate students' learning long-term*?** Responding to this question means applying the selection criteria of *endurance* and utility over time. Examples of skills with staying power include reading comprehension, research, and hypothesis testing.

BOX 2.1. CRITERIA FOR DETERMINING POWER STANDARDS

- Endurance
- Leverage
- Readiness for next grade/course

- **Which standards are *applicable to many academic subjects*?** Addressing this query involves discerning the skills and knowledge with strongest *leverage*. Curriculum improvement teams might include interpreting tables, charts, and graphs, as well as nonfiction writing, in their responses.
- **Which standards denote knowledge or skills *critical to success in the next grade/course*?** This question captures the powerful selection criterion of *readiness* for the ensuing grade level or, in secondary schools, subsequent courses in a sequence. Productive decision-making about readiness can be prompted with variations on simulated scenarios such as the following: "Imagine that I'm a new teacher at your school, and am seeking your advice. I'm teaching in the grade or course prerequisite to yours. (In other words, if you teach sixth grade, I teach fifth; and if you teach Algebra 2, I teach Algebra 1.) What are the skills and knowledge I need to ensure that my students exit with this year, to increase the odds they'll enter your class with what they need to succeed?" Together, the responses to these three questions should result in fewer, more manageable, and more meaningful curriculum goals for teachers and schools. These smaller subsets of state standards are termed *power standards*. Power standards clarify substantive priorities, increase focus, and recognize that some curriculum goals are more important than others.

The process of grappling with consequential questions such as these can build teacher ownership and understanding of the overall school curriculum. Moreover, collaboratively prioritizing goals for student learning can be a robust form of professional development. Prior research identifies collective participation and focus on enriching teachers' content knowledge as best practices for fostering adult learning in schools (Desimone, 2009).

Coordinate Pacing and Formative Assessment

When accomplished well, streamlining curriculum content standards results in mutually agreed upon learning goals for grade levels and courses. Additional strategies can then be used to organize, assess, and bring these power standards to life in actual classrooms. Rettig, McCullough, Santos, & Watson (2003) offer a three-step process for doing so:

1. **Develop pacing guides.** A pacing guide is an outline that chunks the intended curriculum into instructional units and suggested time frames. (See example in figure 2.1.) Whereas power standards focus

Time Frame of Unit	Titles/Content/ Essential Questions	Objectives to Be Included	Implementation Notes
Aug.28-Oct.14	Living Systems • Parts of cells • Classifying How are living things classified? What is a cell?	Use a microscope to make observations of cells. Describe the essential parts of plant and animal cells. Compare and contrast plant and animal cells. Group organisms into categories (five kingdoms of living things, vascular and nonvascular plants, vertebrate and invertebrate animals). Compare and contrast the five kingdoms of organisms.	Reserve projecting microscope. Add pictures to classification key this year.
Oct.15-Nov.6	Structure of Matter What is matter? How does matter change states?	Understand the definition of matter. Determine how heat affects the states of matter. Construct models of atoms, molecules, elements, and compounds. Compare and contrast mixtures and solutions, elements and compounds, and atoms and molecules.	Include unit vocabulary in weekly word study activities.

Figure 2.1. Sample Pacing Guide. (Adapted from Figure 2.1. Pacing Guide [Curriculum Component], Rettig, M. et al. [2004]. Larchmont, NY: Eye On Education, p. 12.)

on fundamentals to be mastered by the *end* of a grade or course, pacing guides address timing and sequencing *within* a school year or semester.

Guidance is the key concept here. That is, in our view, leaders' emphasis should be placed on this tool's potential to *guide*, rather than prescribe, the taught curriculum; to assist, rather than to micromanage, teachers (David, 2008). Since time is a scarce and costly school resource, it makes sense to plan its use purposefully and collectively. Additionally, if most teachers of the same subject are working toward similar unit objectives at about the same time of year, each will have at least one other colleague with whom to consult, share ideas, and resolve common challenges.

Pacing guides may be especially useful for newer teachers, and can serve as a focus for mentors' assistance and support. Understandably, novices may be consumed by planning for individual lessons and single days. Veterans can draw on previous experience to estimate timing and understand how individual units contribute to the bigger picture of a whole year's goals.

2. **Create and administer common assessments.** When similar pacing around powerful learning goals is in place, then context-specific, formative assessments can be designed and used by teams of teachers.

   Creating and administering common assessments can yield several benefits. First, individual teachers gain insight into their own instruction from the process of working with others to decide which knowledge and skills are most important to assess. Second, teachers are exposed to a variety of formats for assessing student learning, as others share ideas for paper-and-pencil unit tests, performance assessments, project-based evaluations, rubrics, checklists of grading criteria, and the like.

   Perhaps most importantly, the administration of common assessments generates a larger set of information about the learned curriculum than can be gleaned from a single classroom. And larger data sets are more amenable to analysis for *patterns* (e.g., strengths, weaknesses, what students "got," what they didn't). These patterns form the basis of a third strategy, discussed next.

3. **Target interventions.** Analyzing the results of teacher-designed, common assessments is a means of regularly opening student work to collective problem-solving. Rettig et al. refer to these collaborations as "staffing meetings" (2003, p. 73). Their purposes are to: (a) scrutinize formative assessment results as a grade-level, team, or department; (b) identify areas where students are struggling; (c) plan appropriate interventions for individuals or groups of students; and (d) refine pacing guides or assessments as needed.

Regular staffing meetings bring the three-step process full-circle, underscoring shared responsibility for student learning throughout. In their work with schools, Rettig et al. (2003) found that, "Over time, staffing meetings become increasingly efficient and manageable; as teachers master this process, it becomes embedded in the school culture" (p. 74). They also emphasize that the principal's leadership, involvement, and support of these processes is critical. Examples of meaningful support include providing feedback, guidance, technical assistance, clerical help, time, and other resources to the grade levels, teams, and departments engaged in this important work.

Design Curriculum Units Backward

Whereas power standards and pacing guides can help focus the curriculum for entire courses and grade levels, common assessments and staffing meetings may be tailored to curriculum units, grading periods, quarters, or other time frames compatible with school goals. A complementary strategy geared to the *unit* level of curriculum planning and assessment is "backward design" (Tomlinson & McTighe, 2006; McTighe & Wiggins, 2004).

Consistent with Ralph Tyler's classic curriculum theories (1949) and Stephen Covey's more recently popular ideas about "beginning with the end in mind," backward design is a three-step planning process. (See figure 2.2.)

- **Clarify top priority student learning outcomes.** The first step involves identifying what may essentially be considered "power standards" for a unit of instruction, rather than for a grade-level or course. That is, teachers think through what they most want students to know, understand, or be able to do by the end of a particular unit of instruction. Typically, instructional units include a range of information, skills, and other possibilities for learning. This unpacking and prioritizing step presses planners to decide ahead of time which are most important. What are the "big ideas" or "essential questions" that should focus teaching and learning in this unit?

    Applying the three criteria elaborated in our earlier discussion of power standards (i.e., endurance, leverage, and readiness, in this case, for subsequent units) can help discern provocative questions and key concepts. These big ideas and essential questions serve as organizing frameworks within which the unit's myriad other facts, concepts, skills, and dispositions can be understood. They also serve as themes that connect and build coherence among the multiple lessons that make up a

Stage 1— Desired Results	
Established Goals:	
• What relevant goals (e.g., content standards, course or program objectives, learning outcomes) will this design address?	
Understanding(s): Students will understand . . .	*Essential Questions:*
• What are the big ideas? • What specific understandings about them are desired? • What misunderstandings are predictable?	• What provocative questions will foster inquiry, understanding, and transfer of learning?
Students will know . . .	*Students will be able to . . .*
• What key knowledge and skills will students acquire as a result of this unit?	• What should they eventually be able to do as a result of such knowledge and skill?

Stage 2—Assessment Evidence	
Performance Tasks:	*Other Evidence:*
• Through what authentic performance task(s) will students demonstrate the desired understandings? • By what criteria will "performances of understanding" be judged?	• Through what other evidence (e.g., quizzes, tests, academic prompts, observations, homework, journals) will students demonstrate achievement of the desired results? • How will students reflect upon and self-assess their learning?

Stage 3—Learning Plan
Learning Activities:
• What learning experiences and instruction will enable students to achieve the desired results? How will the design:
W = Help the students know *Where* the unit is going and *What* is expected? Help the teacher know *Where* the students are coming from (prior knowledge, interests)? H = *Hook* all students and *Hold* their interest? E = *Equip* students, help them *Experience* the key ideas, and *Explore* the issues? R = Provide opportunities to *Rethink* and *Revise* their understandings and work? E = Allow students to *Evaluate* their work and its implications? T = Be *Tailored* (personalized) to the different needs, interests, and abilities of learners? O = Be *Organized* to maximize initial and sustained engagement as well as effective learning?

Figure 2.2. Planning Template with Design Questions. (From *Understanding by Design: Professional Development Workbook* [p. 30], by Grant Wiggins & Jay McTighe, Alexandria, VA: ASCD. © 2004 by ASCD. Reprinted and adapted with permission. Learn more about ASCD at www.ascd.org.)

unit. As with other curriculum priority setting, identifying big ideas and essential questions can help reduce content overload, for both teachers and learners.

- **Identify assessment evidence in advance.** The second step in backward design is to answer the questions: "How will we know when students have achieved the desired results [specified in step #1]? What will we accept as evidence of student understanding and proficiency?" (Tomlinson & McTighe, 2006, p. 28). Another way of framing these questions is, What kind of information will signal that students "got" what we most hoped they would? This step compels us to plan our assessments and evaluation criteria prior to developing lessons for the unit.

    Clarifying in advance what we will be looking for in students' performance can help hone instruction. For example, if teachers anticipate using a rubric to evaluate students' presentations or writing, thinking through the criteria to be employed in the rubric will suggest specifics to emphasize during teaching and guided practice activities. Similarly, advance planning of test questions or quiz prompts will help clarify where the unit should be focused.

- **Plan what teachers and students will do.** The third and final step in designing curriculum backward involves determining instructional activities and learning experiences. The key point in this sequencing is that only *after* learner outcomes and evidence of that learning are clear in the mind's eye should teachers then plan more specifically for the unit.

The reason this design is called "backward" is because teachers more commonly begin their curriculum planning processes by determining instructional activities for a unit or lesson. Only later are assessments constructed or learning standards tied in.

In contrast, experts in the backward model find that it: (a) keeps learner performance and results at the forefront of curriculum planning; (b) helps teachers focus on significant content, rather than opting for broad "coverage"; and (c) inspires development of instructional units designed to enable students to achieve key desired results (McTighe & Wiggins, 2004).

Strategies for Principals

So far, this chapter has described and illustrated several different approaches for improving the intended and experienced curricula. These strategies involve groups of teachers and others working together toward important goals. Obviously, the principal cannot be the one leading every improvement process or facilitating each grade-level and subject area team. Nonetheless, school-based administrative leadership is needed to ensure that the curriculum initiatives undertaken are well-resourced and guided by what we know about best practice. What does such support and guidance look like?

Sharing Leadership

Principals are uniquely positioned at the interface of the school building, the district office, and the broader community (Gupton, 2010; Murphy, Elliott, Goldring, & Porter, 2006). Accordingly, they should have a well-developed sense of which kinds of curriculum decisions would benefit from central administration, parent, student, or other constituent group participation, and which are best made by teams of building teachers and administrators. In most cases, the active involvement of teacher opinion leaders, union leadership, and other respected faculty members can smooth the way for the implementation and longer-term success of any curriculum improvement effort (Wiles, 2009).

That said, because each school context is unique, no universally applicable formula exists for determining optimum composition of the workgroups and task forces needed for the improvement processes described in this chapter. Size of grade levels or departments, teacher and administrator expertise, political considerations, history of community support, traditions within districts, and other variables should factor into principals' judgments about whom to encourage—and which volunteers to okay—to participate in and facilitate such groups.

Fortunately, teacher leaders exist in all schools, and strong principals nurture and purposefully share leadership within their buildings (Bowgren & Sever, 2010; Gupton, 2010; Wahlstrom et al., 2010). Sharing wisely requires knowing one's staff well, including, for example, their:

- **Communication strengths.** Who consistently garners colleagues' attention and esteem when contributing to faculty meeting discussions?
- **Curriculum interests.** Who recently asked to be nominated to the Literacy Collaborative training sponsored by the regional resource center?
- **Academic backgrounds.** Who has completed a master's degree in social studies? Who is about to earn certification as an administrative leader?
- **Team experience.** Who is comfortable collaborating with others on issues of teaching and learning?
- **Community values.** Who is tuned in to the nonmajority cultures and expectations of the school neighborhood and wider community?

- **Leadership skills.** Who facilitates problem-solving discussions well? Who understands our school-wide enhancement goals and how curriculum improvement fits within them?

No matter what the ultimate membership of curriculum improvement teams turns out to be, principals should ensure that professional development in group dynamics is provided for designated facilitators. We elaborate this important support function next.

Training for Group Facilitation

Some assistant principals, department chairs, deans of students, and teacher leaders may be naturally talented facilitators of adult workgroups. Others may have previously been well schooled in interpersonal relationships and group facilitation, perhaps as part of their training as mentors, peer coaches, staff developers, program coordinators, counselors, school psychologists, and the like.

However for designated facilitators with limited prior experience or professional development, principals should allocate funding and time for training in at least the basics of group dynamics. What are some of those fundamentals?

Most experts in group development emphasize a useful distinction between "task" and "relations" roles. Both roles are vital to groups working productively and well. Therefore, it is the facilitator's responsibility to notice when one or the other is missing, and to either fulfill the missing role her- or himself, or see that another group member takes it on (Glickman, Gordon, & Ross-Gordon, 2009).

As the "task" label implies, some roles function to ensure that the job-at-hand is accomplished, that closure is reached, and that the work gets done, ideally within the time parameters predesignated in the group's charge. Task-masters may engage in behaviors such as reminding the group of its purpose, summarizing progress made to date, clarifying issues remaining, and organizing timetables for work completion. Task-masters often bring action orientation, drive, discipline, and efficiency to curriculum improvement processes.

In contrast, relations-oriented roles give higher priority to making sure that interactions among group members are constructive, that conflicts are resolved amicably, and that all members participate and feel good about the process. Relationship-builders may engage in behaviors such as noticing which group members appear confused, angry, or uncomfortable; encouraging reluctant participants to voice their opinions; and affirming others' contributions. These people-oriented roles can help build collaborative spirit, achieve needed compromise, and engender healthy environments within which curriculum group-work can occur.

Meeting Basics

In addition to ensuring that both task and relationships are well attended to, group facilitators require basic knowledge of how to organize and conduct effective meetings (Wiles, 2009). Although it is vital to sustain a climate of inclusion, trust, and respect for all participants, these basics are mainly additional task-oriented functions.

For example, we recommend developing a brief meeting agenda (in outline or bulleted form) and distributing it at least a day or two in advance of the scheduled work session. The workgroup's name, meeting date, start and end times, location, and any expectations for what group members should bring to the meeting are essentials to state at the top of a participant-friendly agenda. (See box 2.2.)

Since group members will want to know why they are being asked to meet, begin the written agenda with succinct specification of the meeting's purpose. If the group facilitator cannot clearly answer the question, "Why are we having this meeting?" then the meeting should *not* occur.

A handy rule of thumb is to express both purpose and agenda items in terms of verbs, to emphasize an action orientation and to signal expectations that time will be used productively (e.g., to brainstorm, to create, to design,

---

BOX 2.2. SAMPLE MEETING AGENDA FORMAT

Sixth Grade Team Meeting
Wednesday, November 6
3:15 – 4:30 p.m.
Conference Room G

Purpose: To finalize rubric for common research paper.

Please bring sample rubrics from October meeting.

1. Review power standards for 6th-grade writing
2. Hear from Amy and Paul on trial use of rubrics D & E
3. Reach consensus on revisions
4. Decide next steps: Who, what, when

to review, to follow-up, to decide, to bring to closure, to finalize, etc.). Some facilitators find that including number-of-minutes next to each agenda item can help keep meetings on track (for example: Introduce tasks, 3 minutes; Activity #1, 20 minutes; Activity #2, 10 minutes; Summarize decisions, 5 minutes; Clarify next steps, 5 minutes). Even if facilitators choose not to include such specificity in writing, thoughtfully anticipating likely timing can help determine what a realistic number of agenda items is for the amount of overall time available for the meeting.

It is often helpful to devote part of an initial meeting to identifying a few participant-generated *ground rules*—that is, expectations for constructive behavior during meetings. Facilitators may find, for example, that most group members value addressing one task at a time, neutralizing conversation dominators, redirecting unproductive discussions to the group's purpose, avoiding redundant debate, and summarizing progress (Wiles, 2009).

Sustaining Concentration on Priorities

Whereas sharing leadership and sharpening group facilitation skills center on process, a key responsibility for principals is to keep collective efforts focused on the school's agreed-upon curriculum improvement priorities. Examples of ways leaders can sustain focus include:

- *Identifying* the substantive charge of workgroups, preferably in terms of useful products. For example: Are teams to develop pacing guides for fourth-grade social studies? To create common assessments for ninth-grade English? To backward design a creative writing unit? To fine-tune a primary literacy intervention already in place? To review assessment data about aspects of the math curriculum students struggle with most?
- *Clarifying* the authority of these workgroups, task forces, and curriculum committees. That is: Are teams' roles advisory? Are they authorized to make final decisions? To generate recommendations? To draft units, planning guides, or assessments that other teachers, administrators, or school boards will consider, revise, or possibly even reject? It is critical to understand boundaries up front.
- *Providing* time for collaborative curriculum work. In addition to capitalizing on regularly scheduled faculty meeting time and professional development days, there are four other ways to make time: (a) schedule common planning time; (b) buy time beyond the work day and school year via stipends; (c) reduce teachers' contact time with students, for example, by hiring substitutes; and (d) bank teachers' contact time with students, for example by extending the student school day for four

days a week—thus depositing time, in banking terms—so that it can be withdrawn on a fifth day, when students either arrive late or leave early, providing time for adult workgroups.

- *Allocating* funds to support curriculum workgroups. Securing supplementary salary for teacher-facilitators may be warranted. Consultants might need to be employed for larger-scale efforts like developing power standards. Subscription to online resources like *ubdexchange.org* cost money; yet their numerous samples and feedback from experts can jump-start school efforts to backward design units and clarify "big ideas" and "essential questions" to focus curricula.

- *Supporting* teacher-facilitators. Principals should attend workgroup meetings as regularly as possible, to provide feedback, underscore the importance of the group's work, and articulate connections to overall school improvement goals. Additionally, when peer-to-peer conflict resolution among group members is unsuccessful, principals need to step in to keep the work moving forward. There may also be opportunities to connect teacher leaders with others in similar roles in neighboring districts and regional educational units.

- *Spelling out* parameters for anticipated timing, work products, and communications. For example: How many common assessments are expected to be administered by when? How frequently will group facilitators update the principal on team progress and needs? Will update reporting be oral or written? How frequently will the principal attend curriculum workgroup meetings to lend encouragement and stay involved? When and how will assistant principals help teacher-led teams?

To build upon the theme of leadership tools for coordinating and enhancing a school's educational program, we turn next to the topic of curriculum mapping.

3

~

When Is Curriculum
Mapping Useful?

The sixth-grade team leader takes a seat across from the principal and says, "I asked to meet with you because I saw you at the school science fair and was wondering if you noticed what I did?" The principal responds, "If you mean that two-thirds of the children's projects were about dinosaurs, I certainly did notice." The teacher adds, "It didn't bother me that so many chose the same topic. After all, dinosaurs sure are interesting to young kids. But I was troubled that they didn't seem to differ much in terms of the science concepts and skills they showed in their work." The principal reflects, "This isn't the first time questions have been raised about how the earlier grades are address- ing our science standards. Maybe it's time for us to take a good look at what's happening in science K–6."

D o tools exist to help schools systematically examine the scope and sequencing of particular subjects across teachers and grade levels? How can such periodic check-ups lead faculties toward better coor- dination and reinforcement of their individual efforts? What can principals do to facilitate and support bottom-up problem-solving that ameliorates cur- riculum weaknesses?

Curriculum mapping is a field-tested strategy useful for tackling these critical concerns.

What Is Curriculum Mapping?

Experts define curriculum mapping in a variety of ways (English, 1980; Hale, 2008; Glatthorn, Boschee, & Whitehead, 2006; Jacobs, 1997, 2004; Ude-lofen, 2005; Wiles, 2009). We think it most useful to understand mapping as *a multiphase process that informs and facilitates collaborative school improvement work by outlining and displaying the taught curriculum.* Before we explain each phase, a few comments on other terms in our definition may help: outlining, displaying, and taught.

Recall from chapter 1 that the taught curriculum is what is enacted by teachers in individual classrooms—as distinct from that which may be idealized, recommended, or hoped for in curriculum guidebooks, state standards, and the like. The focus here is on what actually occurred. For curriculum mapping, individual teachers share what they and what their students worked on during some defined time period.

This sharing, however, is succinct and big picture; hence the verb *outlining.* Teachers sketch out key ideas, essential questions, skills, or other agreed-upon elements of units already taught. Although these sketches require reflection, conceptual clarity, and candor, mapping does not involve describing instruction in depth or generating detailed summaries.

The root of the other verb in our definition, *display,* suggests two additional mapping fundamentals. First, what individuals report is shown to and studied by other teachers. Second, outlines are typically collapsed into table formats of one sort or another, so that information across teachers and grade levels can be exhibited concisely. These chart-like graphic representations partially explain why the process is referred to as mapping.

Other aspects of the mapping metaphor will become apparent as we elaborate the specifics of this curriculum improvement tool. The phases we describe below are drawn directly from the work of a leading expert on curriculum mapping, Heidi Hayes Jacobs (Jacobs, 1997, 2004). (See box 3.1.)

Phase 1: Data Collection

All teachers participate by briefly outlining what they taught over the course of an academic year. Although templates for gathering this information may be tailored to whichever curriculum elements make most sense for a particular school, outlines typically recap:

a. Content addressed (e.g., key concepts, big ideas, essential questions, topics);
b. Skills or processes emphasized; and
c. Assessments of learning (e.g., products or performances).

**BOX 3.1. PHASES OF THE CURRICULUM
MAPPING PROCESS**

1. Data collection
2. First read-through
3. Mixed group reporting session
4. Large group review
5. Deciding on immediate revisions
6. Determining longer-term research and planning
7. Continuous review cycle

Each teacher completes this phase independently.

Since this piece of the process is retrospective, teachers should carry out this work however frequently they need to, to be able to accurately recall the requested information. For example, those accustomed to keeping written daily lesson plans may be able to successfully extract the needed data from quarterly reviews of their lesson plan books. Others may need to set aside time after teaching each day, unit, or week to jot down notes about the content, skills, and assessments included.

Regardless of an individual's system for, or frequency of, recording, teachers will ultimately display their notes in terms of the ten months of the school year. Although mapping experts recognize that instructional activities seldom fit neatly into four-week time frames, months are used as collective reference points, since the calendar is a parameter all teachers have in common. (See figure 3.1.)

In anticipation of this phase of the mapping process, curriculum leaders should share with teachers a variety of possible templates, some blank and some filled in for different grade levels and subject areas. A wide range of formats are available online. We suggest starting at *www.curriculum21.com*, because of the comprehensiveness of links to sample maps, templates, mapping software, upcoming conferences, on-site consulting services, and more. This website represents a division of Curriculum Designers, Inc., a company founded and headed by Dr. Heidi Hayes Jacobs. Its goal is to provide resources and services to schools and others engaged in curriculum mapping. (See box 3.2.)

Different templates can be used to structure, record, and communicate specific aspects of the curriculum that school teams wish to work on. Teachers and administrators can discuss the pros and cons of various formats prior to deciding together which one to adapt or adopt for use school-wide.

Sample Curriculum Map: First Draft

Teacher: Matt Russell   *Course:* ELA Reading   *Section:* 4th grade

	October	*November*	*December*
Essential Questions	What is the difference between nonfiction and fiction? In what ways does a biography tell a story?	How do writers "hook" their readers? What is a document-based question?	How did E.B. White "hook" readers? How can we explain the fact that White's work continues to engage readers?
Content	Biographies: a range of books available for different levels of reading. Students choose independent reading.	Authors' hooks: literary devices, plot structures, openings that engage. Political cartoons.	Metaphors, similes, and analogies; *Charlotte's Web*
Skills	Identifying points of view; distinguishing fact from opinion	Identifying opening lines and titles; writing practice on engaging the reader	Identifying metaphors, similes, and analogies; using metaphors, similes, and analogies
Assessment Type	Research paper demonstrating understanding of the work; spelling test	Three-author essay - - students will identify three authors of their choice and employ corresponding hooks	Identifying key metaphors, similes, and analogies in a chapter of *Charlotte's Web*; interpreting the novel

Figure 3.1. Example of Month-based Data Collection for Curriculum Mapping. (From *Getting results with curriculum mapping* [p. 87, Fig. 7.2], by Heidi Hayes Jacobs [Ed.], Alexandria, VA: ASCD. © 2004 by ASCD. Reprinted with permission. Learn more about ASCD at www.ascd.org.)

BOX 3.2. WEB RESOURCES FOR MAPPING, SAMPLES, SOFTWARE, TEMPLATES, AND MORE

Curriculum Designers, Inc.
http://www.curriculum21.com

Public Broadcasting System
http://www.pbs.org/teacherline/search/?q=mapping

National Education Association
http://www.nea.org/tools/12959.htm

Curriculum Mapping 101
http://www.curriculummapping101.com

Providing ample opportunity to review and deliberate samples before the data collection phase begins:

- Demonstrates respect for teachers as curriculum decision makers;
- Enhances shared understanding of the scope of the work;
- Models the kind of outlining required; and
- Can decrease predictable concerns about do-ability.

We say more about leadership responsibilities and anticipating teachers' concerns later in this chapter.

Most schools today rely on teachers inputting phase 1 data directly into computer templates. However, teachers may also handwrite on index cards, standard sheets of paper, or large newsprint tablets, if clerical help is available to then transfer the information electronically. For reasons that will become apparent as subsequent phases are explained, the process hinges on format consistency across teachers and grade levels.

Phase 2: First Read-Through
Each teacher also conducts this phase independently, starting by reading through the completed templates for the whole school. It is typically best to begin by scanning the overall scope of the maps, to gain general information about colleagues' taught curricula. After a preliminary look at the big picture, teachers carefully re-read and, still independently:

- Underline content, skills, or assessments new to them (e.g., "I wasn't aware you did that!")
- Circle for future collective review and possible revision:
  - Redundancies
  - Gaps
  - Noteworthy assessment practices
  - Matches (or mismatches) with standards
  - Currency (i.e., up-to-datedness)

In this phase, the teacher's task is to identify areas warranting consideration by a larger group, rather than to judge, revise, or make suggestions.

Teachers are expected to bring discerning eyes and critical thinking to these read-throughs, much like editors would. The rationale for conducting this initial editing work independently is to:

- Minimize concern for offending others;
- Decrease the odds of glossing over weaknesses apparent in data displays; and
- Tap the analysis skills of a wide range of professionals.

Phase 3: Mixed Group Reporting Sessions

Now the collective work begins. In groups of six to eight individuals, teachers share the results of their independent analyses. Similar to phase 2, this process is nonjudgmental and non-decision-making. Participants simply take turns reporting out what they underlined or circled (above). A facilitator records participants' findings on large sheets of paper. The desired result is a collective list of areas needing future attention.

This phase is termed "mixed" because these small groups consist of staff members who do not typically work together. For example, teachers should not be placed in groups with colleagues who teach in the same grade level, house, or department, or who team-teach or otherwise partner in the classroom.

The rationale for this purposeful mixing is that "when someone is conversant on a topic, he or she may be too close to the material, read between the lines, and miss critical gaps" (Jacobs, 2004, p. 27). Also, group members who are familiar with each other tend to homogenize maps so they look similar. The goal, instead, is to accurately and publicly record observations about the maps from first read-throughs, with all their similarities and differences.

After mixed-group reporting sessions conclude, group facilitators meet together and compile all findings onto larger charts, by grade level, subject area, or other categories that make sense for a particular school. These charts become the main subject of the next step in the mapping process.

Phase 4: Large Group Review

The charts produced in the previous phase are clearly posted or projected around the meeting room. This phase may be facilitated by the principal, a teacher leader, or other skilled professional internal or external to the school.

All faculty members participate by reviewing the posted findings and identifying patterns. The patterns noted may center on content, skills, assessments, gaps, repetitions, or other findings. Facilitators record the patterns of findings for all to see.

As this phase concludes, the mapping process is poised to shift from analysis and review to curriculum revision or development. If the school is small (10–25 teachers), subsequent phases may be undertaken as a whole faculty. Otherwise, workgroups should be organized by instructional units that make the most sense for the school (e.g., grade-levels, primary and upper elementary groupings, departments, or other standing teams).

Phase 5: Deciding on Immediate Revisions

Based on the patterns surfaced in the previous phase, workgroups collaborate to address the curriculum issues that can be resolved through the most straightforward of adjustments, revisions, and negotiations. For example, at times, conspicuous redundancies or unwarranted overlaps can be handled through some simple communications and compromises among a few faculty, teams, or administrators. The public nature of phases 3 and 4 is meant to facilitate the resolution of such issues because problem areas become apparent to the whole faculty.

Also, not all patterns will be problematic. Recall that phase 1 of the mapping process includes identifying unfamiliar practices, noteworthy assessments, and matches with standards (e.g., "We didn't know your team was doing that!"). So, deciding on immediate revisions may sometimes mean, for example, intentionally replicating or adapting a performance assessment used in the fifth grade by fourth-grade teachers. The content in the two grades will be distinct; however, using similar performance assessment techniques can be beneficial.

Obviously, however, not all revisions and needed interventions will be uncomplicated. Hence, the next step in the mapping process.

Phase 6: Determining Longer-Term Research and Planning

The patterns surfaced through collective examination of curriculum maps may lead workgroups to identify problem areas that involve multiple grade levels, schools, structures, or policies. For example, will formal essay writing be introduced at the elementary or the middle school? Does exclusive focus on creative writing in one grade put students at a disadvantage for the nonfiction writing emphasized at the next grade level? What skills or concepts seem to be misplaced and might better be taught at some lower or higher level?

Maps facilitate examination of the logic, sequence, and flow of conceptual and skill development over time. "Articulation" and "vertical alignment" are terms sometimes used to refer to such logic or flow from one grade, course, or school to the next. "Horizontal alignment" typically refers to coordination of content and skills within the same grade level or across multiple subjects.

These larger and more complex vertical and horizontal alignment issues are as important to address as the immediately resolvable, smaller-scale ones. Principals' involvement, leadership, and communication with district administrators will be especially needed for these situations. Often, it will be beneficial to convene curriculum task forces to conduct additional research, explore options, and create solutions. The information gathered about the taught curriculum for the mapping process can provide useful starting points for task force work.

Whether handled in phase 5 or 6, the goals for immediate and longer-term improvement through mapping are to:

- Fill in gaps
- Eliminate unwarranted repetition or duplication
- Ensure the curriculum advances upward in complexity
- Address power standards
- Update curriculum and assessments

These problem-solving phases are vital pieces of the mapping process. Revisions can result in adding to or subtracting from the overall "volume" of the curriculum (Wiles, 2009, p. 77). Refinements can make the experienced and the intended curriculum more congruent with one another (English, 2000). Modifying the scope and sequence of what students encounter can make school experiences more coherent for them.

Phase 7: Continuous Review Cycle

As the multiple phases described above make clear, mapping takes time. Follow-up to what the maps display leads to additional curriculum refinements or adjustments. Moreover, faculty turnover occurs, and state standards and local community expectations for schools change over time.

Because the taught curriculum continuously evolves, attending well to its coordination and strengthening should also be ongoing. For all of these reasons, curriculum mapping is not a "once and done" strategy but, rather, part of a re-curring cycle of action research, analysis, and collaborative problem-solving.

The Value and Benefits of Mapping

In chapter 2, our emphasis was on how leaders help *focus* curricula. The school curriculum was viewed through close-up lenses. That perspective allowed us to zoom in on micro-level improvement strategies such as design-ing curriculum units backward, developing common assessments and pacing guides, and streamlining standards.

In contrast, curriculum mapping is a tool that facilitates wide-angle views of curricula and systemic, macro-level improvement interventions. Clearly, big-picture and close-up perspectives complement one another. But what, more specifically, are the benefits and value of mapping?

Substance

Perhaps distinct from what is written in curriculum guidelines, mapping provides "real-time information about the actual curriculum" (Jacobs, 1997). Accordingly, mapping enables improvement work centered on what students encounter in the classroom: the taught curriculum (English, 2010). Authen-tic portrayals of the whole of students' experiences can help schools better coordinate the parts (Wiles, 2009).

Timing

Curriculum maps provide general information about the amount of time spent on particular content and skills (English, 1980). Maps also shed light on the specific order in which ideas and processes are addressed. Information about time and sequencing can point to adjustments necessary to make more sense to learners or to increase concentration on agreed-upon priorities. Ad-ditionally, since the amount of time dedicated to a particular topic or skill is an indicator of the degree to which it is prized, curriculum maps provide tangible representations of a school's values.

Transparency

Because all faculty members have access to the same teacher-generated data and displays, mapping can increase school-wide awareness of problem areas and thereby decrease resistance to implementing changes. Moreover, because these data-gathering, review, and problem-solving phases are essentially bottom-up processes, they are distinct from traditional management approaches in which administrators assess and define the changes to be made.

Communication and Adult Development
The varied phases of mapping provide opportunities to grow professionally through:

- Reflecting on one's own teaching
- Gaining insights into colleagues' taught curricula
- Learning where one's own contributions fit into the bigger picture of students' experiences
- Engaging in research-informed collaboration and decision-making that directly affects students

Like the strategies elaborated in the previous chapter, mapping is another means of working together to improve the taught and experienced curricula. The initial phases of data collection, outline collation, and display are essential groundwork. However, the real value to learners comes from the creative problem-solving and curriculum modifications prompted by collective sense-making of the maps. The ultimate benefit (and goal) is increased curriculum coherence for students.

Additional Strategies for School Leaders

For already-busy teachers immersed in nurturing their "own" classrooms every day, addressing school-wide curriculum coordination is not likely a front-burner concern. Leadership is needed, therefore, to periodically turn collective attention to the big picture of students' experience across teachers, grade levels, and subject areas.

What else can principals do to increase the odds that mapping will lead to macro-level school improvement?

Establish Need
A first step is to share with teachers any indicators that suggest incipient problems with curriculum coordination or alignment. For example:

- Does this chapter's opening vignette about unwarranted redundancy in science topics apply to other subjects in your school?
- Has the principal been receiving a growing number of parent complaints that their children "already did the Civil War" *last* year?
- Do test item analyses of standards-based state exam results suggest gaps in student development of a particular kind?

- Are new teachers privately questioning the value of a whole grade-level production or field trip, even though veterans assure them "we've been doing this for years and the kids get a lot out of it"?
- Have teachers at receiving schools been noticing up-ticks in student weaknesses in a specific subject or skill area?

Mapping may be an appropriate approach if multiple signals such as these regularly surface, or if the smaller-scale strategies described in chapter 2 prove insufficient.

More systemically, a need for curriculum mapping might emerge from root-cause analysis of top priority school quality issues. Root-cause analysis engages faculty and administrator teams in probing carefully and thinking creatively to discern what may really lie beneath, for example, students' less-than-desirable performance. In most cases, multiple factors contribute to significant gaps in student learning (Killion, 2002; McTighe & Thomas, 2003; Tallerico, 2005), only some of which center on the coordination and alignment of the taught curriculum.

For example, some contributors to key problems may have to do with district policies: How, if at all, does the zero-tolerance fighting policy relate to at-risk students falling farther behind? Other factors may point to school structures: Are support systems available in time to intervene and remediate early difficulties in reading? Some factors will center on the students themselves: Are our poorest essay writers those adolescents who have the worst attendance in the middle grades? If so, then what is at the root of many of those absences, and has the school fully exploited community partnerships that can increase attendance?

Other factors may have to do with instructional materials: How does the biology text we adopted address the gap we have identified in our students' science knowledge? Some factors will relate directly to the staff's current knowledge and skills: How familiar are our teachers with varied instructional strategies that foster the kinds of student problem-solving required on today's state exams? Have adequate time and funding been devoted to professional development in that area? And, of course, some factors may point directly to the curriculum: Is there a mismatch between what is tested in third-grade arithmetic and the taught curriculum for that grade?

When curriculum mismatches or lack of coordination and communication about the taught curriculum are determined to be important root causes of subpar student learning, then mapping can be beneficial. Mapping should not be undertaken, however, simply because schools in neighboring districts are doing it, or because a popular consultant presents mapping as *the* solution for low test scores.

As our description of phases showed, mapping thoroughly and well is a labor-intensive process. Teachers may be motivated to participate constructively if they receive clear explanations, up front, about the issues mapping is intended to resolve in their particular school. In short, principals must first establish the need for curriculum mapping, before requesting that teachers take part.

Articulate Rationale
In addition to substantiating need in a particular school, leaders must also be prepared to articulate the broader rationale for curriculum mapping. In other words, part of addressing the "Why are you asking us to do this?" question involves being well-versed in the value and benefits of mapping. As elaborated earlier in this chapter, mapping can lead to better curriculum coordination, improved communication among staff and, most importantly, increased coherence for students (Jacobs, 1997, 2004). Principals need to be able to communicate the value of eliminating unwarranted redundancies and addressing curriculum gaps, as well as of other benefits summarized earlier.

Moreover, articulating rationale is a leadership responsibility throughout all phases of the process, not just at the start. In any ambitious improvement initiative, there will be dips in performance and plateaus in energy levels (Fullan, 2007). Principals can help faculty advance beyond these inevitable ups and downs by reminding workgroups of what the school is trying to accomplish, how each phase contributes to the success of the next, and where a particular group's curriculum efforts fit into the bigger school improvement picture. Principals' active and enthusiastic participation in all phases of the mapping process adds power to verbal reminders.

An important aspect of providing sound rationale for mapping involves addressing teachers' concerns about the possible intrusiveness of data collection. Since the first phase of mapping centers on teachers sharing their taught curricula, some will be nervous about whether that information will be used against them in some evaluative way (e.g., Is the administration trying to catch me teaching something I shouldn't be, or omitting some content or skill for my grade or courses? Will my teaching be judged inadequate when I outline the order in which I approach a particular unit?).

In anticipation of these predictable concerns, principals should assure teachers that there are no ulterior or punitive motives for gathering information about what was taught. School leaders need to emphasize how important it is that data collection brings to light what teachers and students actually engaged in, rather than what teachers think administrators want to hear about their classrooms (Jacobs, 1997, 2004; Udelofen, 2005). The latter subverts the entire purpose of authentic display and analysis of the taught and experienced curricula.

Facilitate Interventions

Although principals' involvement, guidance, and support are important to all stages of mapping, leadership may be most crucial in its problem-solving phases. For example, at the smaller-scale resolution level of phase 5, some teachers or grade levels might not want to add or "let go" particular concepts, essential questions, assessment activities, authors, or genres, even though mapping evidence suggests they should. Principals can help find common ground, reconcile differences, propose compromises, or otherwise exercise influence, all toward the goal of optimizing students' overall curriculum experience.

At phase 6, where more complex structural and systemic issues are addressed, principals' leadership is essential to solutions that involve altering a school's master schedule, reconfiguring teaching teams, and funding new materials acquisition, professional development, or investigation of interventions implemented in similar schools in other districts. Additionally, mapping evidence may uncover possibilities for interdisciplinary (cross-subject) curriculum partnerships; principals would be key to building in common planning time for such alliances to thrive.

Principals would also do well to facilitate leadership roles for the school's library media and available instructional technology (IT) specialists. Given these specialists' associations with teachers and technology, they can bolster mapping work in a number of ways. Media and IT specialists bring unique expertise in accessing resources to support varied curricula, locating new instructional materials, and working with computer software of different types. Since they often have experience helping teachers become comfortable with new media, they may be able to smooth the path during the data entry phases of information gathering. Similarly, in review phases, library media and IT specialists can be encouraged to take lead roles in exploiting electronic search capabilities for collaborative curriculum analyses. Heidi Hayes Jacobs offers the following examples:

> Perhaps the key word "rain forest" is put into the computer to find all places in the school curriculum where that subject is taught. Working with curriculum maps, the computer identifies seven places K-12 where the word appears. . . . With the advent of standards, teachers in a building may want to search the district map for a type of assessment such as "bar graphs" to see if they are developed with sufficient complexity from elementary through

high school mathematics classes. There is also the real possibility that the computer might identify no entries for a particular key word. This highlights a glaring gap. If a task force finds nothing on "critical thinking and television," they've now identified an area for development. (1997, p. 43)

A number of these examples involve multiple schools within a district. These cases highlight another important leadership role for principals: that of advocate and key communicator for their school. When several schools need to cooperate to find curriculum solutions, principals will often serve as one of a few building representatives to district-wide problem-solving groups. Representing a school well necessitates deep understanding of the school's educational program, faculty, and students. It also requires the ability to communicate effectively and, at times, persuasively, on behalf of school priorities and interests.

Notwithstanding principals' key communication roles, sharing leadership with teachers and support staff remains critical to the success of mapping and other curriculum improvement work. In part, this entails the principal modeling active listening, optimism, and constructive problem-solving in groups. It also means cultivating teachers' creativity and voice. Means of doing so include fostering climates in which faculty feel safe expressing opinions contrary to those of administrators. Other means involve welcoming teachers' questioning of the status quo and encouraging teachers' ideas for addressing mismatches surfaced during mapping. As discussed in chapter 2, providing time for communication and collaboration is vital to each phase of the process.

Caveats

School leaders should enter the curriculum mapping process with eyes wide open. Although its benefits are substantial, mapping requires considerable time and effort from all faculty, as well as meaningful and sustained support from administrators. Moreover, in part because of longstanding traditions of teacher autonomy in the classroom, the disclosure, transparency, and analytic critique the process relies on may not seem "natural" or comfortable for many.

The research-based recommendations included in this and previous chapters will go far to address and ameliorate these challenges. Nonetheless, it is also important to understand a fundamental criticism of this and other strategies aimed at closely aligning the taught curriculum. Michael Apple, a renowned scholar, refers to such aims as "deskilling" teaching (Apple & Beane, 2007). His term is intended to underscore that tightly delimiting, prescribing, and standardizing teachers' and students' work can serve to disempower and alienate faculty. Critics of tightly aligned curricula point to the benefits, instead, of teachers' and students' imagination, improvisation, curriculum flexibility, and "productive idiosyncrasy" (Eisner, 2001, p. 368).

Supporters of curriculum mapping counter such criticisms by emphasizing that mapping focuses on *what* is taught, not *how*. They point out that faculty members maintain the freedom to decide the teaching strategies, techniques, and activities to be used to facilitate learning in their classrooms. (We revisit these and other fundamental differences in curriculum philosophies in chapter 7.)

Like any educational tool, of course, the quality and purposefulness of its use will ultimately determine whether potential benefits are realized. Mapping is no different. Its overall goal is a taught curriculum that is organized and enacted in a way that builds on what came before and fits together well, so as to be clear and coherent for learners. It is a wide-angle instrument that can supplement other curriculum improvement tools in a leader's repertoire. Additional ideas for enhancing that repertoire are elaborated next.

4

~

What Are Other Curriculum Support Strategies?

You've served as principal for three years now, and the new personnel director pulls you into a meeting at the district office. She begins: "We've drafted most of the copy for our advertisement of the principalship vacancy at Sunnyside. I'd like to pick your brains about what else we should include." You read: "Instructional leader needed for grades 6–8 middle school. Strong communication skills and current knowledge of best practices in curriculum and instruction required. Professional development experience preferred."

You wonder if anyone in the meeting will ask, "Don't we also want someone with strong organizational ability and know-how about managing buildings, materials, and schedules? Curriculum and instruction covers an awful lot of ground. What are some practices we would want candidates for this position to be familiar with? And, what kinds of professional development experiences are known to be most effective?"

These questions underscore how connected curriculum leadership is to both ongoing adult learning and skillful management of operational supports.

Why Administration Is Important to Leadership

First, some comments on key vocabulary. The phrases educational *management* and *administration* have fallen out of fashion in recent decades, in favor of expressions emphasizing educational *leadership* in its various forms (for example, instructional leadership; leadership for learning; learning-centered leadership; transformational leadership). Sometimes, instructional leaders

47

are contrasted and compared to educational managers, with the latter either explicitly or subtly framed as the lesser of the two (e.g., Erickson, 2007, p. 120). It is as if unspoken modifiers are meant to accompany these supposedly lesser roles; that is, *mere* managers or, worse yet, *traditional* administrators.

We recommend more even-handed acknowledgment of the reality that schools (and organizations generally, for that matter) require both strong leadership and effective management. Put another way, skillful management and administration are essential *pieces* of successful leadership, although insufficient by themselves (Hewitt, 2006; Wiles, 2009). This perspective is supported by educational research indicating three main ways in which principals influence student learning: by setting direction, by developing human resources, and by making the school organization work (Leithwood, Louis, Anderson, & Wahlstrom, 2004; Murphy, Elliott, Goldring, & Porter, 2006; Wahlstrom, Seashore Louis, Leithwood, & Anderson, 2010). The third way captures a number of important managerial roles and administrative responsibilities.

Let's start by illustrating more specifically what "making the organization work" means for school curricula.

Managing Recurring Operations Smoothly

Earlier in this book, we spoke to the need for principals to:

- Provide time for teachers to collaborate on curriculum priorities
- Allocate funds to support curriculum workgroups and teacher-facilitators
- Schedule and assign students in ways that enable, rather than impede, the intended curriculum
- Make clerical help available to ease mapping procedures
- Put teacher-friendly systems in place for acquiring or sharing instructional materials and supplies
- Update and maintain the school's electronic technologies

Many of these recurring responsibilities are part of what we introduced as the supported curriculum. Two additional management and maintenance functions underscored by curriculum expert Jon Wiles (2009) follow.

Communications Systems
Building leaders often receive information about state or national curriculum and assessment changes, emerging issues, research updates, grants, and other curriculum-related mandates and opportunities, as channeled through

district offices or superintendents. Accordingly, principals need to establish routines for: (a) reviewing such materials; (b) deciding which merit dissemination or delegation to faculty/staff and which require culling into more easily digestible formats; and (c) ensuring that relevant curriculum and assessment information is forwarded to the appropriate personnel in a timely way.

School leaders are wise to consult with faculty and teacher association/ union representatives about preferred means of conveying, offering feedback, and capitalizing on district, state, and national curriculum communications. For example, some schools may have success with hard-copy postings on bulletin boards in common areas; others might opt for electronic discussion boards, shared computer folders, or text-messaging alerts linked to where new information can be located.

Ideally, systems would be adaptable to communications in multiple directions; that is, from the principal to faculty, as well as from faculty to the principal and others. When it comes to matters of curriculum and assessment, teachers and other support staff often belong to professional organizations particular to their interests and areas of expertise. These specialized sources of information can be quite different from those that typically reach building principals. Examples of specializations include the Music Teachers National Association (*www.mtna.org*), the Council for Exceptional Children (*www.cec.sped.org*), the National Association for the Education of Young Children (*www.naeyc.org*), the National Association for Bilingual Education (*www.nabe.org*), the International Reading Association (*www.reading.org*), and many more. These professional organizations typically stay on top of emerging issues, state-of-the-art research, and field-tested programs particular to their curriculum niches. Hence, they can be valuable resources for schools' curriculum improvement work, especially when systems are sustained to keep colleagues well-informed.

Data Management

Systems also need to be maintained and continuously upgraded for other kinds of curriculum-relevant information. Today's principals should have user-friendly electronic storage and record keeping arrangements in place to:

- Share the power standards, pacing guides, formative assessments, rubrics, backward-designed units, and curriculum maps discussed in earlier chapters
- Retrieve Individualized Educational Plans (IEPs), so that support personnel and teachers can obtain information about particular students' learning, curriculum, and testing modification needs

- Monitor students' grades, attendance, and disciplinary histories, so that timely curriculum interventions can occur as patterns emerge
- Facilitate the development and use of teaching portfolios and portfolios of students' work
- Aggregate data required for accreditation reviews or curriculum audits
- Analyze students' standards-based assessment data associated with school and district benchmarks, literacy levels, state requirements, and the federal No Child Left Behind Act (NCLB)

Although ease of access to these kinds of information will influence whether and how they get used, *where* data are stored electronically typically matters less (e.g., at district offices, regional services centers, school servers, or elsewhere).

Textbook Adoption

Another recurring responsibility requiring skillful management is the adoption of texts and other curriculum materials. Even where statewide textbook adoption is the norm, districts typically can select from among a list of state-approved books. Also, although many districts adopt district-wide, others allow school-based choice, particularly when school neighborhoods differ greatly (for example, by languages spoken in the home or other distinctive patterns of student need). And, of course, it is not uncommon for individual schools within a district to have one or more unique programs that warrant text or materials adoption. For all of these reasons, adept management and coordination at the building level are essential.

The following six guidelines are adapted from House and Taylor's (2003) recommendations for smoothing the acquisition of curriculum materials (see box 4.1). They note that, whereas individual contexts will vary widely, attention to these steps can help in most situations.

1. **Familiarize yourself with district and state adoption policies.** Policy parameters may specify criteria for evaluating textbooks, software, or other curriculum materials. Some policies may require opportunity for public review of materials under consideration for adoption. Guidelines may be different for required versus supplemental texts. Also, in some cases, union contracts may specify how or when teachers are expected to be involved in adoption processes. Since the cost of materials can be a considerable portion of instructional budgets, it is understandable why some boundaries may be delimited in policy. Typically, local governing boards need to approve adoptions and expenditures.

BOX 4.1　EXAMPLES OF QUESTIONS TO GUIDE MATERIALS' REVIEW PROCESSES

- How well do content and approach match school improvement priorities?
- To what degree do materials align with state and local standards or assessments?
- Are the texts' recommended approaches supported by research?
- Are materials developmentally appropriate for grade levels being considered?
- What about reading levels?
- Is content up-to-date and relevant to today's students' interests and needs?
- Will substance, tone, and visuals engage learners?
- To what extent are cultural and other biases minimized?

---

2. **Draft a timeline.** Work backward, from the date by which materials would need to be received by your school in order to be used effectively in a particular semester or year. Factor in realistic time periods for shared decision-making committees to review and compare materials from various publishers; for teachers to familiarize themselves with the delivered materials prior to being expected to use them in their classrooms; for professional development opportunities aimed at demonstrating, modeling, and addressing teachers' questions about the materials; and for the other steps delineated here. Be sure the timeline takes into account predictable budgeting and purchasing cycles.

   If a timeline is developed at the district level, principals should scrutinize it carefully and advocate for revisions necessary to ensure workability at the school. "The process of acquisition is complex, often involving many people and taking place over a lengthy period" (House & Taylor, 2003; p. 539). Timelines can help manage this complexity and keep the overall process on track and doable for individual schools.

3. **Involve the right people in the review.** The same issues and principles for sharing leadership detailed in chapter 2 apply to working with committees to assess new instructional materials. Useful starting points are to share the draft timeline with those to be involved in the process and to incorporate committee members' insights into a revised version. A

consensus timeline can facilitate shared commitment to keeping pro-cesses moving forward.

Before soliciting samples or inviting publisher representatives to overview resources for a committee's consideration, evaluation criteria should also be agreed upon. That is, just as you would prespecify required and preferred qualities desired in prospective applicants when advertis-ing a position vacancy for your school, it is equally important to identify in advance what the curriculum team is looking for in materials to be considered for adoption.

If the school committee is obliged to use certain district or state criteria, it may be possible to add to or tailor those parameters to school-particular needs and goals. The school curriculum priorities, power standards, curriculum maps, and common assessments recommended in earlier chapters are logical sources from which to derive selection crite-ria. Revisiting school vision and mission statements, as well as any other documents that articulate intended curricula, should also help. Early attention to these ideals should facilitate review and culling processes.

4. **Solicit and examine references.** Additional sources of useful feedback for decision-making teams are teachers and principals from other schools and districts who adopted the materials in recent years. Experienced users should be able to speak to students' engagement with the materi-als, their value to teachers, the quality of the professional development provided by the publisher, whether or not the publisher was reliable in meeting delivery deadlines, and most importantly, what, if any, effect the materials had on students' learning. If the publisher cannot or will not provide such references, that may also be important feedback for the committee to consider. Of course, insights from references are most valu-able when their student populations are similar to those of your school.

5. **Pilot test materials in classrooms.** After possibilities have been nar-rowed to two or three top contenders, it is wise to support committee members' and others' firsthand trial testing of materials. Respected teacher-opinion leaders and faculty who volunteer are typically good choices for the trials. Additionally, publishers are sometimes willing to provide consultants to teach your students with their materials, while faculty observe. Be sure to pilot accompanying resources as well as main texts (e.g., assessments, teaching manuals, visual aids, electronic supplements). Also, ensure that sample materials are made available to any grade-level or course teacher who wishes to examine them. If the content of any of the materials might be considered controversial, or if their instructional approaches represent significant departures from past

practices, ensure effective communication with students' families as well. Feedback from trial runs and multiple constituents' perspectives should inform the selection committee's recommendations to the governing board for official approvals.

6. **Negotiate with publishers.** Clearly, the larger the potential order, the greater the leverage to be exercised in negotiations. For large orders, consider everything negotiable, including shipping costs, supplementals, and amount of consulting time to help teachers become better acquainted with all the features of the materials. For orders of any size, obtain guarantees in writing and include financial penalties for late delivery. As mentioned in our discussion of timeline development, be sure delivery dates allow generous amounts of time for teachers to study the new materials, engage in professional development focused on the new curriculum, plan lessons, and otherwise prepare for optimizing use of new resources (see box 4.2).

We conclude our discussion of materials adoption with a qualification. We have situated this information among administrative routines because numerous management tasks are involved in materials' acquisition, and because textbook adoption is sometimes a relatively straightforward process aimed at updating older resources.

However, materials' adoption also presents the prospect for leaders to influence student learning, because textbooks can significantly shape the taught and experienced curriculum. "The purchase of new curriculum materials presents an opportunity for school leaders to exercise considerable leverage on student learning. Moreover, the acquisition of materials is much simpler and more direct that other ways to improve student learning" (House

---

BOX 4.2. SIX STEPS FOR ADOPTING AND ACQUIRING NEW CURRICULUM MATERIALS

- Become familiar with district and state adoption policies.
- Draft a timeline.
- Involve the right people in the review.
- Solicit and examine references.
- Pilot test materials in classrooms.
- Negotiate price, delivery dates, and professional development services.

& Taylor, 2003, p. 538). For these reasons, we position this responsibility at the intersection of our discussion of principals' routine management responsibilities and learning-centered leadership roles.

Leading for Learning

Although managing a school's curriculum is important and complex, it is only one element of leadership for student learning and well-being (Hewitt, 2006; Murphy et al., 2006).

> Effective curriculum leadership does all of those things [discussed above] plus establish new direction, align people and resources, motivate participants, and produce meaningful change for school improvement. In short, effective curriculum leadership is more than maintenance, it is dynamic in nature. (Wiles, 2009, p. 1)

What is involved in establishing new direction, honing human resources, and implementing change for the better in schools? We turn to these questions next.

Setting Direction

In earlier chapters, we discussed two key aspects of direction-setting: collaboratively establishing priorities and keeping collective efforts focused on those priorities. We described processes for facilitating deliberations and making decisions about what the curriculum should emphasize, include, and leave out. We underscored the need for perseverance and support to ensure that changes resulting from prioritizing have the chance to take hold and flourish.

Streamlining content standards and designing curriculum units around big ideas and essential questions, were among the strategies suggested for focusing curricula in desired directions. In chapter 7, we will elaborate on how educational philosophy and political leadership also shape vision and help establish direction.

The world constantly changes, research offers new insights, and learner and community interests evolve over time. Hence, leadership entails anticipating and being responsive to emerging needs, as part of direction-setting. Creating new or upgrading existing educational programs are means of addressing that evolution, to prepare students for life in the future. Similarly, moving beyond minimum state standards and required NCLB assessments also often necessitates fresh or revised curricula (Wiles, 2009).

Developing New Curricula

Several of the strategies presented in chapters 2 and 3 are readily adaptable to creating educational programs that serve new directions. For example, applying the principles of backward design includes: (a) beginning with the end in mind by clarifying top priority outcomes intended for the initiative, (b) identifying in advance what will be considered evidence of having achieved those desired results, and (c) then planning the scope and substance of the new program or curriculum (Tomlinson & McTighe, 2006).

Similarly, a now-classic approach to curriculum development known as "the Tyler rationale" frames program design in terms of four guiding questions:

1. What educational purposes should the school seek to attain?
2. What educational experiences can be provided that are likely to attain those purposes?
3. How can these educational experiences be effectively organized?
4. How can we determine whether these purposes are being attained? (Tyler, 1949, p. 1)

In addition to backward design and the Tyler rationale, mapping is another systematic process that can be adapted to new curriculum development. The adaptation primarily requires modifying the first phase of the mapping process delineated in chapter 3 so as to be prospective—planning what is intended for the future—rather than diary-like—capturing the current taught curriculum (Glatthorn, Boschee, & Whitehead, 2006).

Thus, phase 1 would entail determining what teachers, leaders, and other relevant constituents think *should* be taught or included in the new program. Harkening back to power standards, the criteria of endurance, leverage, and readiness could help planning groups reach consensus on these "shoulds."

Teams might also find it useful to consider other criteria and questions compatible with new directions and desired outcomes (see box 4.3). For example, the criterion of relevance: To what extent does a suggested design feature address the challenge or opportunity we are trying to address through this new program? Or, the criterion of student-centeredness (Parkay, Hass, & Anctil, 2010). For example: To what extent will the suggested feature engage and motivate students? To what extent will it relate to students' preferred learning styles or other needs?

Some experts refer to the explicit application of student-centered design criteria as "double alignment" (Strong, Silver, & Perini, 2001). This idea means matching curriculum and instructional strategies with desired/

**BOX 4.3. ADDITIONAL QUESTIONS TO GUIDE
NEW CURRICULUM OR PROGRAM DEVELOPMENT**

- How will school-level changes fit into broader district and state systems?
- Which grade levels and personnel will be included?
- How will others contribute or be involved?
- What materials will be needed to implement the new program?
- What is a reasonable timeline for implementation?
- Who will oversee the program's continuation?
- When and how will intended outcomes be evaluated?

---

standards-based outcomes *while* giving equal consideration to children as learners. Double alignment reflects values that leaders should ensure remain at the forefront of creating and revising programs. These values are relevant whether curriculum improvements are approached via forward mapping, the Tyler rationale, backward design, or any other shared decision-making model.

Because curriculum improvement involves planned change, and because supporting teachers' on-the-job learning is an important part of facilitating change processes, we turn our attention next to leading professional development.

Developing People

What does recent research suggest matters most to teachers' professional development? Five main features are: (1) emphasis on content knowledge, (2) coherence, (3) duration, (4) collective participation, and (5) use of active learning strategies. What, more specifically, do these effectiveness features entail (Darling-Hammond, Wei, Andree, Richardson, & Orphanos, 2009; Desimone, 2009; Garet, Porter, Desimone, Birman, & Yoon, 2001; Tallerico, 2005)?

Focus on Content Knowledge

Focusing on content means targeting a staff development activity on a specific subject area or on a subject-specific teaching method, such as increasing teachers' understanding of motion in physics or of the way elementary students solve story problems in mathematics (Birman, Desimone, Porter, & Garet, 2000, p. 30).

This research finding contrasts with commonplace practices that focus on generic instructional strategies such as using cooperative groups, computer technology, or concept maps in the classroom. It is consistent, however, with the increased expectations for student learning reflected in contemporary curriculum standards. For example, state and district standards often expect higher-level thinking of students and abilities to apply, rather than simply recall, information. Accordingly, educators require deeper understanding of particular curriculum content and how students best learn that content. When the latter becomes central to professional development, participants' knowledge and skills increase.

Enhance Coherence

A second feature of effective professional development is school-wide coherence. In this context, synonyms for coherence are "connection," "complement," and "fit." But what should professional development complement, fit, or be connected to? Two elements:

- Curriculum standards and assessments, as well as school direction and priorities; and
- The substance of previous professional development initiatives, so that adult learning is experienced as a cumulative and recursive enhancement of prior knowledge.

Just as strong teachers link their current instruction to what came before and what is expected to follow on children's learning path, strong leaders ensure that the foci of adults' development opportunities are logically consistent with one another. In this respect, professional learning coherence is similar to the vertical alignment that schools work hard to achieve in curricula for children. Both require keen awareness of and attention to connecting today's learning to yesterday's and to what is anticipated for tomorrow's. Both also require enough content overlap to be *reinforcing*, but not so much as to become redundant.

Increase Duration

Longer duration contributes to staff development effectiveness in two ways. First, duration increases opportunities to digest, try out, and reflect upon new learnings. Second, increased duration facilitates the incorporation of other effectiveness features; for example, *depth* of subject-matter knowledge and *reinforcement* of coherence. The value of longer duration applies to the professional development activity itself and the time span during which follow-up is supported and integrated with other improvement initiatives. This finding parallels the research on time-on-task for students: more is better than less, assuming, of course, that what learners spend their time on is high quality.

Foster Collective Participation

Professional development has also been found to be more effective when teachers participate in it with grade-level or subject-area colleagues from their school. Such participation contrasts with staff development structures in which teachers from different schools participate individually (for example, in district-wide staff development, off-site institutes or academies, college course-taking, etc.). Instead, school-based collective participation can beget sharing and problem solving around common concerns, goals, students, and curriculum.

Collective participation centered on shared hopes and challenges can also enrich school culture more broadly. This happy by-product relates directly to contemporary aspirations that schools function less like bureaucracies and more like professional learning communities (DuFour, Eaker, & Burnette, 2002). Such communities shift development goals from emphasis on individual growth to increased *school capacity* for improvement and renewal.

Use Active Learning Strategies

Complementing strong subject matter focus, enhanced coherence, increased duration, and collective participation, effective professional development practice is also characterized by opportunities for teachers' active learning. This finding is consistent with research on training that demonstrates that hands-on practice is essential for the transfer of new skills to classroom use. Examples of active adult learning strategies include discussion, application exercises, simulations, reviewing student work together, role playing, observing or being observed teaching, joint planning, reciprocal mentoring, peer coaching, and team-created presentations, demonstrations, or other written products.

Now the question becomes: How can these five research-based insights guide school leadership? (See box 4.4.)

Set and Sustain Fewer Priorities

After carefully investigating the ways in which schools address the problems of limited teacher time and fragmented professional development, Watts and Castle (1993) concluded that "Sometimes it is better to slow down, accomplish more by attempting less, and accept the fact that you can't do it all" (p. 309). As discussed in earlier chapters, current expert

---

BOX 4.4. FIVE FEATURES OF EFFECTIVE PROFESSIONAL DEVELOPMENT FOR TEACHERS

- Emphasis on content knowledge
- Coherence
- Duration
- Collective participation
- Use of active learning strategies

---

thinking echoes that earlier research by underscoring the value of persistent leadership focus and priority-setting. For many schools, that means concentrating on fewer improvement goals, including those for teachers' professional development.

> Schools stumble when their leaders cannot identify priorities, or when they seem to say "Pay attention to everything; everything is important" . . . . Six school improvement goals are not better than one. Meaningful substantive changes in schools occur through focused, concentrated efforts. (DuFour, 2002, pp. 60–61)

It is more difficult to trim initiatives than to expand them. But trimming is sometimes needed for a school to be able to address selected priorities deeply and well. Concentrating attention on fewer goals can be a significant means of stretching scarce time and funding strategically, while also reducing overload, increasing coherence, and enhancing duration.

Stress Students' Subject-Specific Needs

What should be the content of teachers' professional development? The answer is short and straightforward: *the curriculum*. More specifically, those parts of the curriculum that students struggle with most. The focus is what children experience every day in classrooms—the taught and tested curriculum.

Where would the adults in schools be concentrating attention if their professional development centered on those parts of the curriculum that students struggle with most? As discussed in chapter 2, one focus is common formative assessments. Another is staffing meetings wherein grade-level teams or departments plan appropriate interventions for individuals or groups of students, based on those assessments.

A third source of adult learning content centered on children's priority needs is the actual work that students create. Such work takes myriad forms, including written responses to problems they are asked to solve, science lab results, videotapes of presentations they make, exhibits they produce, projects they complete, writing samples, portfolios in various subject areas, or any other products resulting from assignments and class activities.

Similar to the backward-designed units and common assessments discussed earlier, these work samples become the heart of teacher discussion and problem solving about how to improve student learning (Langer, Colter, & Goff, 2003). Student work related to the standards and learning goals considered essential for a particular grade level or subject area may be the best kinds of examples to start with. Initial questions for group deliberation might include: What essential skills and knowledge does this work sample demonstrate? What weaknesses or gaps in knowledge does it illustrate? What evidence of ability to synthesize information appears in this sample? What do these samples suggest students are struggling with most?

Although each question directs attention to students' work, connections to curriculum and instruction logically follow. What are some ways in which the teacher's prompts can bring out higher-level thinking? How could the assignment be altered to inspire greater student creativity? What additional support does this child need? How might we change the course syllabus to address recurring weaknesses that appear in these samples?

Incorporate Helpful Protocols and Structures

Clearly, not all grade-level or subject-area teachers will have experience productively discussing student work or developing common lessons and assessments. Nor will all groups have a history of fruitful problem-solving around student underperformance. In these cases, experienced group facilitators and more structured processes to guide curricular dialogues are required (Richardson, 2001). Numerous discussion protocols for examining student work and studying lessons together are available online (see box 4.5).

What many of these ready-to-use protocols have in common are guiding questions to help group members stay focused on describing and improving the work—rather than judging it or nitpicking. Typically, discussion protocols also specify sequences of procedures so as to ensure active listening and turn taking, to better capitalize on all group members' insights. All are aimed at actively engaging participants, clarifying and deepening teachers' thinking, and fostering collaborative and constructive problem-solving around issues important to student learning.

**BOX 4.5. WEB RESOURCES FOR DISCUSSION
FACILITATION PROTOCOLS**

Looking at Student Work
www.lasw.org

Turning Points Tools, Tuning Protocols
http://www.turningpts.org/tools.htm

Coalition of Essential Schools, Resources for Teacher Learning
*http://www.essentialschools.org/pub/ces_docs/resources/sd/teach_coll/
teach_coll.html*

Where to Now?

Although there is no simple answer to the question of which support strategies will work best for your school, savvy curriculum leaders have a wide
range of options at the ready. To complement the technical-rational approaches emphasized so far in this book, we turn our attention next to more
organic models of curriculum improvement.

5

~

Where Do More Integrated
Models Come In?

A member of your school's shared decision-making team asserts: "Am I the only one who feels like social studies and science keep getting pushed aside? The state's focus on ELA and math seems to take more and more of our attention." Another teacher pipes up, "You can add art, music, and health to the list of what's been getting short shrift lately, if you ask me." The literacy team coordinator reacts: "It's not all peaches and cream for us either, you know. The pressures seem to grow each year. We can't keep carrying this load by ourselves."

How might school curricula be organized to lessen disparities that position different subject areas as haves and have-nots in today's schools? What can be done to ameliorate the fragmentation that often ensconces school subjects into separate silos? What strategies can leaders use to increase programs' relevance and coherence for contemporary students?

Two points for school leaders to keep in mind when addressing these and related questions are:

- Integrated curricula can yield important benefits, and
- Such curricula take various forms.

Differing Mental Pictures

So far, we have overviewed leadership strategies commonly acknowledged as best practices for contemporary curriculum and school improvement. Many of these approaches are essentially *linear*, in that they emphasize vertical and horizontal articulation, subject area mapping, and other carefully engineered systems for coordinating learning as students move from one grade level or course to the next.

The benefits of such methods are that, when implemented well, they can increase curriculum coherence for learners and provide helpful guidance for teaching. This vision of coherence may be captured by an image of a ladder or staircase, where orderly, stepwise progressions facilitate both students' and teachers' trajectories toward schools' higher aims.

However, critics of linear models point out that, since work challenges and life opportunities are seldom neatly divided by subject matter, *integrated*[1] curricula can be a means to more authentic coherence for students. To integrate means to join together, connect, mix, combine, or incorporate. When applied to curriculum, integration refers to planned connections among two or more subjects (for example, the disciplines of language arts and history; or mathematics and visual arts). Thus, integration contrasts with the more usual *discipline-based* curriculum in which knowledge is organized and engaged in "separate subjects in separate time blocks during the school day" (Jacobs, 1989, p. 14).

A potential benefit of integrated approaches is that they may help streamline overcrowded educational programs. As Gordon (2004) explains, given today's environment of ever-increasing expectations for schools:

> [I]t is absolutely impossible to *add on* all of this desired content to the existing curriculum! Only by folding basic competencies into larger, more meaningful learning experiences can educators hope to develop a teachable, learnable curriculum. . . . To meet state mandates while creating meaningful learning opportunities, several competencies can be integrated within a single theme, problem, or project. (p. 241)

Experts also suggest that cross-subject collaborations can unleash teachers' creativity (Drake, 2007; Jacobs, 1989), at times a welcome and needed prospect, given current pressures for standardized curriculum and centralized assessment. From this perspective, a tree, with its intertwining leaves, branches, and roots, provides a visual model quite distinct from the ladder or staircase imagined earlier, portraying the more organic forms that integrated curricula can take. What, more specifically, do those different forms look like?

Variations of Integrated Curricula

The term *integrated curriculum* has evolved to encompass quite varied degrees of connection. The distinctions that follow are drawn from the work of internationally known expert Susan Drake (2007), supplemented by other sources where specifically noted (see figure 5.1).

Fusion

In fusion models, a particular set of skills, concepts, or content is incorporated into an existing discipline-based curriculum (see figure 5.2). Examples include introducing:

- Reading comprehension skill development into other subjects taught in elementary grades, such as social studies, science, and mathematics.
- Character education concepts (such as honesty, respect for differences, and personal or civic responsibility) into all subjects taught at a middle school.
- Global studies into every department at the high school level; for instance, by adding:
  - Required readings by authors from countries other than the United States
  - Multinational interpretations of history, the arts, and sport
  - International perspectives on current events or popular culture

Fusion provides a means of emphasizing an agreed-upon idea, message, or skill set across diverse disciplines. Entire books and periodicals have been devoted to implementing fusion thoroughly and well; for example, the *Writing Across the Curriculum* journal and Harold Herber's classic volume, *Teaching Reading in Content Areas* (1978). Fusion may be applied district-wide, school-wide, or across selected subject areas and grade levels.

Fusion may also be extended to extracurricular initiatives such as parent engagement, school–community partnerships, and athletics. For example, Benjamin Franklin Middle School (Ridgewood, New Jersey) so highly values cooperation over competition in its school-wide social and emotional learning efforts that it instituted a no-cut policy for its sports teams. All children can participate, and Benjamin Franklin fields no "elite" team when it plays other schools (Drake, 2007, p. 32).

Overall, in this model, typical disciplines (subject areas) remain intact, with new or additional skills, concepts, or content suffused into them. For this reason, the added-in content may be thought of as secondary to the main subject, at least to some extent.

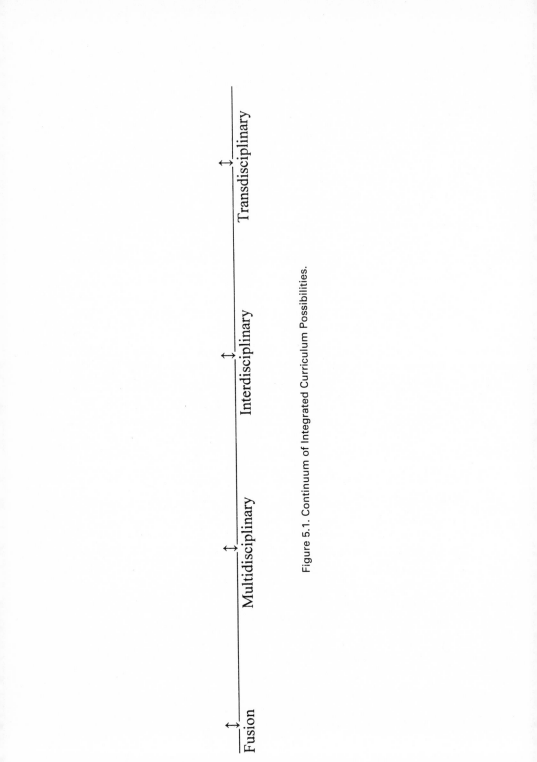

Figure 5.1. Continuum of Integrated Curriculum Possibilities.

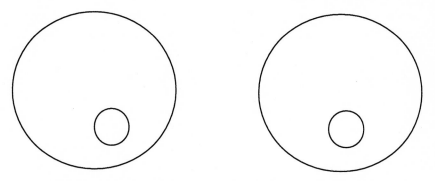

Figure 5.2   Fusion: Separate Subjects with Other Content Added.

Multidisciplinary

Subject areas also remain distinct and intact in the multidisciplinary model. However, in contrast to fusion, here, there are typically no identifiable main and secondary partnered subjects. Accordingly, the multidisciplinary model is sometimes referred to as *parallel* or *coordinated* curriculum (see figure 5.3).

Gordon (2004) offers the following illustration:

> [D]uring the same month, a science teacher teaches about space travel, the English language arts class reads and writes stories about space travel, and the math class learns about measurement by solving problems focused on space travel. (p. 242)

Drake (2007) illustrates that, at the secondary level, teachers or departments may organize a multidisciplinary curriculum, so that students read *The Red Bad of Courage* in their English course (a novel about the experiences of a young recruit during the American Civil War), while concurrently studying that war and related sociopolitical concepts in their history class.

Similarly, within a single classroom at the elementary level, a lesson or unit might focus on developing skills of prediction. Children might be expected to rotate among different subject-specific learning centers and small groups. In the math center, students practice predicting the next number in differently patterned sequences (e.g., What number would come next in the pattern: 16, 17, 18 . . . ? Next after 2, 4, 6, 8 . . . ?). In the language arts center, students are asked to forecast what might happen in an unfinished story, before moving on to learn what the author actually wrote. At the art center, they draw a picture of their predicted story line. After watching the teacher demonstrate an experiment in the science center, children are asked to predict what will happen in their own subsequent, related experiments.

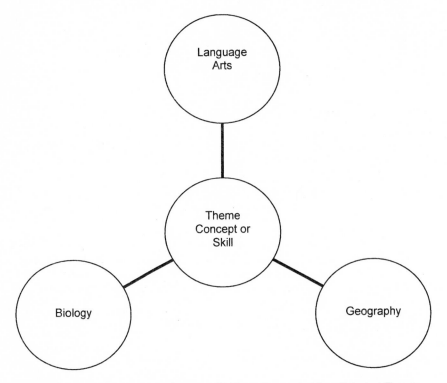

Figure 5.3. Multidisciplinary: Separate Subjects Connected to a Selected Theme.

(Students' predicting abilities could be refined at the secondary level, via lessons paralleling this elementary illustration in different departmentalized courses rather than in distinct learning stations within a single classroom.)

As these examples illustrate, multidisciplinarity often centers on a common *theme, context, or skill*, approached from distinct disciplines. The instructional purposes of such coordination include mutual reinforcement of selected skills/themes (e.g., prediction, space travel) or richer understanding of a particular context (e.g., the U.S. Civil War era). In addition to these conceptual connections, multidisciplinarity also typically involves common *timing* across separate subjects, with teachers of different content teaching related units at about the same point in the semester or year.

Interdisciplinary

Whereas the multidisciplinary model largely reflects *synchronization* of distinct subject areas, interdisciplinary curricula involve deeper and more frequent blending of two or more disciplinary perspectives. Accordingly, interdisciplinarity requires regular (rather than intermittent) co-planning by teachers who bring different subject area knowledge to shared lesson and unit development. Sometimes, team teaching is the model of choice for interdisciplinary work.

For example, rather than scheduling students into separate social studies, English, and arts classes at the secondary level, a Humanities team might develop and jointly teach an entire semester's curriculum, during an expanded block of co-taught time. In this way, students experience learning in a less fragmented, more integrated way, with different teachers serving as primary facilitators or resources, depending upon the concepts or skills addressed and the questions students or teachers raise.

Interdisciplinary curricula are typically organized around a common theme or issue. Big ideas are connected *across* subject areas instead of *within* them (see figure 5.4). Appropriate themes must be broadly significant and of sufficient richness that the different disciplines can be brought to bear in meaningful ways.

In the Humanities example mentioned above, the themes of conflict, leadership, or change might prove fertile conceptual underpinnings for exploring literature, politics, economics, history, music, and more. For math and science interdisciplinary collaborations, curriculum themes might revolve around broad skill sets such as collecting, graphing, charting, and

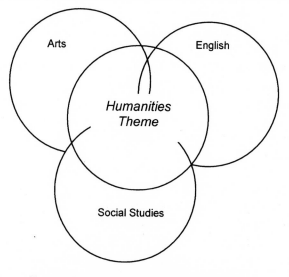

Figure 5.4. Interdisciplinary: Multiple Subjects
Overlapping Around Organizing Theme.

analyzing data. Curriculum standards for the respective grade levels can shape the particular skills and ideas that drive the lessons and units addressing the agreed-upon theme(s).

Transdisciplinary

For the three versions of integration summarized so far, the knowledge base of various disciplines (subjects) are key starting points for organizing themes, collaborations, and curricula. Moreover, effective fusion, multidisciplinary, and interdisciplinary teachers typically articulate and emphasize cross-subject connections, rather than assuming that all students will discern, notice, or make the connections among the disciplines for themselves.

In contrast, for the highest degree of integration—*transdisciplinary*—the ideal is for separate subject boundaries to completely fade into the background. Instead, curriculum and instruction foreground issues, problems, or questions of interest and relevance to students themselves. Thus, the starting points for transdisciplinary curricula are contemporary, real-world concerns and students' curiosities, rather than concepts and skills considered central to either separate or deliberately linked subject areas.

What might this kind of integration look like in practice? Teachers confident in their knowledge of a particular group of students' interests can anticipate relevant and timely organizing topics. Other teachers may prompt student brainstorming of real-world problems or issues they'd like to learn more about. Topics that surface might include violence and bullying, environmental sustainability, or teen alcohol use.

With teachers' additional probing and guidance, topics are typically translated into researchable questions. Experts in transdisciplinary approaches note that children and youth can and do raise substantive questions, often related to personal growth and broad social concerns (Beane, 1997). For instance:

- How can the world become a more peaceful place?
- Where does food come from?
- How has oil become so important to the world?
- What does the future hold for me?
- Who has power, and how is it exercised?
- Why do some athletes and musicians make lots of money?

Teachers then help students prioritize or collapse themes and decide whether to address common interests as a whole class or in smaller groups. Some may agree to tackle several main questions over the course of the school year. Others may divide up questions by teams of students within the class. Usually, students and teachers together generate related subquestions to guide investigations into and learning about the main one.

Obviously, the nature and scope of questions are keys to ensuring rigor and value for the emerging curriculum, as well as its feasibility. This aspect of the curriculum-shaping process requires similar thoughtfulness to what was discussed in chapter 2 as the role of *essential questions* and *power standards* in guiding teaching and learning.

Once focusing questions are established, skills, concepts, and knowledge from the different subjects are introduced or retaught as warranted. For example, pursuing answers to the sample questions bulleted above would necessarily involve research skills, reading and vocabulary development, mathematical computations of various sorts, social studies and science concepts, and historical, political, and economic content. Thus, information from the disciplines is linked to and *serves* the questions asked or problems addressed, in an on-demand or as-needed basis.

This approach to subject matter content contrasts with the other degrees of integration described earlier in this chapter. Essentially, the question of "Which comes first, relevance or subject matter?" is turned on its head in transdisciplinary integration. That is, most of us work hard to make the substance of what we teach relevant and interesting to students. A transdisciplinary approach would have us concentrating first on what's relevant and interesting to today's students, then bringing our substantive expertise to those interests. Often, this approach involves teachers learning alongside students, less-predictable outcomes, and more emergent rather than pre-planned learning activities.

For all of these reasons, transdisciplinarity represents the most distinctive—and least frequently implemented—level of curriculum integration in most educational settings. Related applications of this approach are elaborated when we address additional alternatives to discipline-based curricula in the next chapter.

Overall Sense-Making

As Jacobs (1989) reminds us in her influential work on integration, at its heart, curriculum improvement is creative problem-solving. A school curriculum's enduring "problem" is how to organize and engage the knowledge, skills, and dispositions important to children's development and well-being. Integrated curricula provide pathways for overcoming the challenges of information overload and subject-centered fragmentation that sometimes contribute to this fundamental problem. Integration can also increase the curriculum's relevance and provide stimulating, authentic experiences for students. Hence, it is an aspect of curriculum leadership worth knowing.

It's also important to understand that, although we compare and contrast four variations above, integration is best thought of on a *continuum* of degrees of possibility. In fact, some theorists identify six, eight, or ten different levels or types of integrated curricula (see, for example, Jacobs & Fogarty, cited in Drake, 2007, pp. 28–30).

Furthermore, varying degrees of implementation inevitably occur *within* the four models recapped in this chapter. The frequency and quality of cross-subject connections will fluctuate by classroom, teacher, and teams. And, of course, the seamlessness of integration will differ greatly, depending upon teaching expertise, quality of professional development, collaboration styles, leadership facilitation, time, and material resources. We turn next to more specific implications for principals.

Leadership Strategies

As Drake's (2007) extensive fieldwork with teachers and administrators underscores, integration can address required standards as successfully as discipline-based approaches, when mindfully attended to during curriculum planning. In fact, many of the same leadership strategies elaborated in chapters 1–4 are equally applicable to integrated curriculum development and implementation. That is, both are most effective when coupled with:

- Streamlined content standards
- Essential questions or big ideas
- Clear school priorities for student learning
- Resource allocation to support those priorities
- School-wide norms of teamwork and community
- Training for selected teacher-leaders
- Research-based professional development practices
- Time to collaborate

What are additional leadership implications particular to integrated curriculum?

Knowing When Integration Can Be Fruitful

As mentioned in chapter 3, curriculum mapping can uncover high-potential prospects for cross-subject partnerships and integration. That is, when mapping makes apparent where and when highly related concepts or skills are currently being addressed, it may make sense to develop multidisciplinary learning units across those subject areas. Such parallel coordination may require only minor adjustments to teachers' sequencing of existing lessons and units. Thus, multidisciplinarity may be a means of taking advantage of redundancies, rather than eliminating them.

Additionally, in circumstances when funding scarcity or other political realities marginalize content the local school community values, interdisciplinary curricula offer a way to promote well-rounded opportunities for students. For example, given contemporary emphases on the frequently tested basics of English language arts and mathematics, the visual and performing arts, health, wellness, and children's physical development are often short-changed (Gordon, 2004). Integrating the latter with other subjects can be a means of stimulating children's multiple intelligences, while also sustaining disciplines that would otherwise be neglected.

Capitalizing on Informal Relationships

In virtually every school, friendship groupings and professional affinities naturally occur. Without any social engineering, pockets of teachers share ideas, seek each other's counsel, support one another, and collaborate to resolve mutual challenges. When those informal bonds form across separate subject areas, tuned-in principals may find them fertile ground for *piloting* integrated curricula. The idea is to make the most of existing collaborations, start small, and buoy experimentation dependably.

Whether fledgling integration experiments succeed or fail, there will invariably be much to learn from initial forays. How the principal treats outright and partial successes, as well as stumbles, will shape subsequent curriculum change. The grapevine can be counted on to spread word about the extent of the principal's support and the trailblazing teachers' thoughts about whether integration was worthwhile.

Incipient successes with sufficient leadership backing can prompt other teachers to volunteer to create and try out integrated units at other grade levels or across other constellations of subjects. As Gordon (2004) points out:

> Teachers who previously have not participated in developing integrated curriculum could start by getting assistance from colleagues in integrating

some simple content from other disciplines into the courses they teach. Next, teachers could begin to coordinate courses, first for one or two units during the school year, and eventually for the entire year. Interdisciplinary teams can begin more comprehensive integration with a few thematic units of instruction, and eventually move to integrated curriculum throughout the school year. (p. 243)

When a critical mass of early adopters emerges, it may then be appropriate to identify a teacher-leader or small task force to ensure continuation of initial momentum (Glatthorn, Boschee, & Whitehead, 2006). The charge for such a task force can include determining next steps for professional development, for scheduling time to collaborate, or for addressing other unanticipated needs.

Critically Analyzing Selected Themes
Most variations of integrated curricula center on teacher-identified or students-and-teacher collaboratively generated themes. Because these decisions are so central to the questions, units, and learning opportunities developed around them, themes need to be robust and meaningful (Drake, 2007). Accordingly, the same care and creativity should be applied to theme development as chapter 2 suggested for *essential questions* and *power standards*.

A reasonable starting point is to extrapolate big ideas from required content, standards, and school improvement priorities (Gordon, 2004). To increase relevance, students can be encouraged to surface themes from local community concerns, national or global current events, and issues that are interesting or puzzling in their own lives.

To avoid superficial or trivial themes, teacher collaborators or teacher-guided classroom lessons can test preliminary thoughts by creating *concept webs* that display relationships among big ideas, subthemes, and questions (Glickman, Gordon, & Ross-Gordon, 2009; Gordon, 2004; Jacobs, 1989). If a web appears "thin" or quickly leads to dead-ends, the theme may not be sufficiently rich or complex to serve well as an integrated curriculum organizer.

In figure 5.5, Jacobs (1989) provides an example of a concept web developed around a substantively rich theme (flight) and the related essential questions:

1. What flies?
2. How and why do things fly in nature?
3. What has been the impact of flight on human beings?
4. What is the future of flight? (Jacobs, 1989, p. 59)

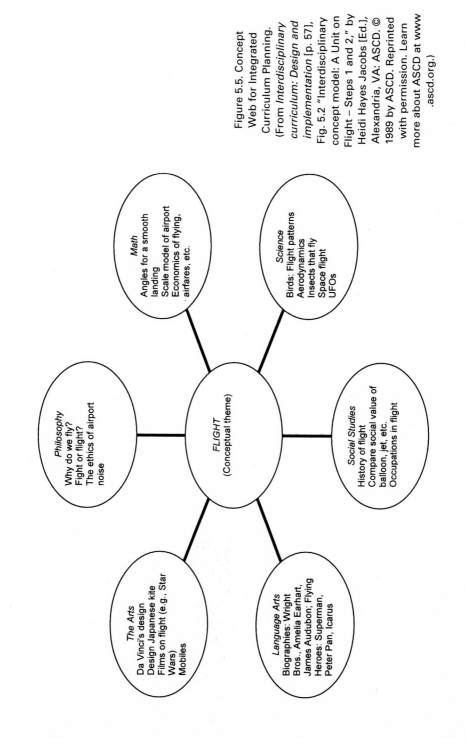

Figure 5.5. Concept Web for Integrated Curriculum Planning. (From *Interdisciplinary curriculum: Design and implementation* [p. 57], Fig. 5.2 "Interdisciplinary concept model: A Unit on Flight – Steps 1 and 2," by Heidi Hayes Jacobs [Ed.], Alexandria, VA: ASCD. © 1989 by ASCD. Reprinted with permission. Learn more about ASCD at www .ascd.org.)

Math
Angles for a smooth landing
Scale model of airport
Economics of flying, airfares, etc.

Science
Birds: Flight patterns
Aerodynamics
Insects that fly
Space flight
UFOs

Philosophy
Why do we fly?
Fight or flight?
The ethics of airport noise

FLIGHT
(Conceptual theme)

Social Studies
History of flight
Compare social value of balloon, jet, etc.
Occupations in flight

The Arts
Da Vinci's design
Design Japanese kite
Films on flight (e.g., Star Wars)
Mobiles

Language Arts
Biographies: Wright Bros., Amelia Earhart, James Audubon; Flying Heroes: Superman, Peter Pan, Icarus

Where does administrative leadership come in? Principals can:

- Provide professional development focused on concept web development, including hands-on practice and collaborative review of themes
- Convene study groups that include teachers with integrated curriculum experience, to share expertise and offer feedback on novice teachers' and students' incipient theme ideas
- Connect teachers with educators in other schools or districts who were earlier adopters of integrated approaches
- Raise thoughtful questions with experimenting teachers and students; for example:
  - How is this main theme a *stretch* beyond what students already know?
  - Could the theme be modified to broaden the social concern at its heart?
  - Which big ideas from other disciplines might enrich your draft web?
  - What insights has our consulting special educator shared about these subquestions?
  - How are you thinking about this web as a blueprint for next steps?
  - What additional resources do you need to move forward and try out this integrated unit?

Paving the Way with School Publics

Educational leaders need to expect that questions and concerns may arise whenever curricular or other school improvement initiatives differ from students' and parents' prior learning experiences. Since integrated curricula may fall into this category, principals should be prepared to serve communication, boundary-spanning, and buffering roles, to support teachers' implementation. Leadership strategies for this important function include:

- *Being well-informed* about the themes, subject areas, processes, teaching approaches, and projects participating teachers are implementing in their classrooms. Be clear in your own mind about how the integration initiative connects directly to learning priorities for student development and well-being.
- *Articulating* repeatedly the rationale behind and benefits of integrated curricula. Do so for both internal and external audiences, in whatever in-person forums may be part of school and district norms, for example, at parent–teacher organization events; school board, faculty, shared decision-making team, and teacher union meetings; grandparent or senior visiting days; and the like.

- *Sharing* information, updates, and student success stories related to integrated curriculum initiatives via print and other media. These may be school newsletters to parents and community constituents; your school's website or blogs; and local newspapers' education sections. Underscore concrete examples of educational benefits.
- *Creating* and cataloging responses to Frequently Asked Questions, as part of the school's web presence. Checking in regularly with teachers and students engaged with integrated curricula will help identify patterns of questions and concerns that parents, caregivers, and others may have.
- *Enlisting* participating teachers' help in communicating the value of cross-subject integration to their students. Besides contributing to students' understanding, such messages can also make their way to families and help build support for integrated curricula.
- *Building* a strong case with the superintendent and other district leaders, to obtain the resources classrooms need to implement the curriculum well. Support requests with solid rationales for how integrated curricula add value to children's learning and the school's overall program.

In sum, the principal's advocacy matters. Part of effective leadership for learning today means building political and financial support by sharing up-to-date knowledge about promising curriculum practices. This chapter offers the fundamentals needed for that work.

Flexing Schedules and Facilities Use

Principals' management skills also come into play because modifications to schedules and facilities use may be needed to help integrated approaches thrive.

For example, planning time for collaborating teachers is essential. Moreover, whereas common planning time may have previously been organized exclusively *within* subject-area specialties, integration requires *cross-subject* connections. (See chapter 2 suggestions for providing time for teacher collaboration.)

Often, the project-based activities characteristic of interdisciplinary and transdisciplinary curricula can benefit from modified arrangements of *students'* learning time as well. For example, an elementary school might extend a math or English language arts block from 60 to 120 minutes, to foster instructional approaches that integrate additional subjects.

Similarly, modifications to how a school's facilities are scheduled and allocated can foster cross-disciplinary partnerships. For example, increased space might enhance a Humanities co-teaching approach, perhaps combining two or more classes and taking advantage of larger school spaces like cafeterias and auditoriums. Alternatively, contiguous classrooms, perhaps with collapsible walls, might be targeted for prioritized use by participating teachers.

As we move ahead to explore additional alternatives to conventional curriculum practices, we extend several ideas introduced in this discussion of facilitating more integrated models.

Note

1. We use the term *integrated* purposefully. As explained in the ensuing section, the more common term *interdisciplinary* reflects just one of several possible levels or degrees of curriculum integration.

6

~

What About Alternatives to Standardized Curricula?

You're preparing to meet with the assistant superintendent for your annual performance evaluation. You come to items on the Principal's Self-Appraisal form about "addressing diverse student learning needs," "encouraging innovation," and "creating supportive learning environments for all students." As you reflect on how to respond, a nagging concern resurfaces in your mind: I know we're not reaching everyone, especially kids most vulnerable to dropping out of school. What else might we do to serve all our students well?

This leader's reflection suggests awareness that school improvement efforts invariably address some learning needs better than others. What might alternatives to commonplace curriculum leadership approaches look like at both the elementary and secondary levels? What is the thinking behind why such alternatives may be especially warranted at this moment in time?

Another Look at Standards-Based Schooling

The general train of thought characterizing education policy and K–12 curriculum improvement practices over the past several decades goes something like this.

- Subject-specific standards provide frameworks for defining what students should know and be able to do.

- Regularly assessing student achievement of those standards produces useful information for educators' planning and public accountability.
- Achievement can be enhanced by aligning the taught and tested curriculum, and by articulating and synchronizing curricula across grade levels and courses.

As chapter 5 emphasized, integrated curricula offer alternatives to commonplace practices of moving children through programs structured around discipline-based silos.

However, other curriculum experts underscore steeper downsides of predominantly linear, technical-rational approaches to content, instruction, and assessment. Disadvantages include:

- A narrowed, basics-oriented curriculum that hyper-values test taking and constrains teachers (Apple & Beane, 2007; Au, 2007).
- Discernible morphing over time, from standards-driven to *standardized* curricula (Eisner, 2001; Goodlad, in Wolk, 2010).
- Standardization's neglect of both whole-child development (Covey, 2009; Gordon, 2004) and education's transformative potential (Anyon, 2005; Greene, 1985).

Socially Valued Educational Outcomes

Some evidence suggests that subject-centered curricula and their concomitant standards-based assessments rarely reflect the kinds of learning results that educators, communities, and employers highly prize. For example, Gordon's (2004) research finds that, when teachers, parents, or other community members are asked to identify what would characterize the ideal graduate of their K–12 school system:

> Invariably, the composite list goes beyond "basic" content knowledge and skills to include thinking skills, social skills, moral virtues, interpersonal skills, and all of the characteristics cited in the literature on holistic curriculum. (p. 238)

Similarly, when Covey (2009) asked business leaders and parents what they wanted from schools:

> They responded that they wanted students who were responsible, who showed initiative, who were creative, who knew how to set goals and meet them, who got along with people of various backgrounds and cultures, and who could resolve conflicts and solve problems. Interestingly, not one

parent in any focus group said anything about academics or higher test scores—not one. (p. 61)

This research on valued educational outcomes is consistent with popular school mission statements about the nurturance of life-long learners and the development of the "whole person."

So, how to advance societal interests in well-rounded graduates and simultaneously ameliorate the downsides of standardized curricula? One response centers on *personalizing* education, as an antithesis to schools operating like assembly lines with one-size-fits-all curriculum and assessment. Another alternative melds child-centered personalization with theme-based school culture building. A third approach extends transdisciplinary curricula to local community development and broader social reforms. We begin by explaining and illustrating what is currently meant by personalization.

Making the Curriculum Personal

In simplified terms, personalization is to curriculum what differentiation is to instruction (although the latter has garnered more attention among practitioners and publications in recent years). For differentiated instruction, faculty adapt their teaching and modify expected student products to better address children's diverse needs, abilities, readiness, or preferred learning modes (Gupton, 2010; Sprenger, 2003). Although all learners work on the same standards-based content, teachers alter *how* they engage different groups of students with predetermined curriculum substance.

Similarly, personalization involves adaptations and modifications for diverse groups of students. However curriculum *substance* and school *structures* also change. First and foremost, the curriculum becomes more child-centered, rather than standards-focused. As Wolk (2010) explains:

> Students play a significant role in designing their own curriculums, which usually emphasize real-world learning. Teachers become advisors who guide students in educating themselves, tutor them, and help them manage their time and energy. Student learning is assessed on the basis of actual work, as demonstrated in portfolios, exhibitions, special projects, experiments, recitals, and performances—real accomplishments rather than abstract test scores. (p. 3)

Although this description parallels what was characterized in chapter 5 as transdisciplinary curriculum integration, personalization involves additional structural reforms as well.

Personalized schools are usually middle and high schools without rigid schedules or typical academic courses. Most frequently, they are geared to "those youngsters who are least well served by the conventional system" (Wolk, 2010, p. 3). Some operate as stand-alone buildings; others as schools-within-schools. Some are charter schools, and others are options among public school alternative programming.

Essential, however, is that "personalized schools must be relatively small so that students and teachers know one another well" (Wolk, 2010, p. 3). On the one hand, elementary schools are routinely structured to foster close, sustained student–teacher relationships—through traditions of assigning a group of children to a primary teacher for an entire academic year, or for two to three years, in the case of "looping" models. In contrast, time and structures for sustained relationship-building are much less routine at the secondary level. Hence, small size is a key distinction of personalized middle and high schools.

Big-Picture Learning

A concrete example of personalized curriculum is found in *big-picture learning* (BPL) schools. The following BPL description draws mainly from Littky and Grabelle (2004), Washor and Mojkowski (2006), and Wolk (2010).

BPL schools cap enrollment at 150 students. They organize students into groups of no more than 15 per "advisor." Advisors are teachers who serve as learning facilitators, coaches, and educational generalists, rather than subject-matter specialists. An advisor works with the same cohort of students through its four years of high school. As part of their role, advisors develop partnerships with parents, other caregivers, and community-based intern mentors.

Mentors are crucial because the BPL curriculum is grounded in year-long Learning Through Internship (LTI) opportunities and students' individual learning plans. That is, rather than relying on common sequences of subject-centered courses, each student designs her or his own personal curriculum and goals, in consultation with an advisor, parent, and mentor from the community. Students spend two days per week interning with a local organization or business, under the supervision of a workplace mentor. Internships might include authentic experiences in hospitals, government offices, nonprofit agencies, law firms, restaurants, factories, art galleries, and other venues as varied as local community resources allow.

As in the transdisciplinary model described earlier, knowledge and skills from academic subjects are introduced, taught, or applied as needed to serve individual student interests and needs. Interests are expressed as self-identified learning goals. Needs emerge from internship workplaces and personal situations, as well as from special talents that parents and caregivers help point out.

Overall, BPL curricula are based on the premise that students will learn, "remember, and be better able to apply knowledge they gain through authentic experiences" (Wolk, 2010, p. 4). Field-based projects and research conducted throughout internships are designed to benefit both the individual student and the internship site. To graduate, students are also required to complete a senior project and a 75-page autobiography.

Approximately 60 BPL programs currently operate in the United States, most in high-poverty, urban districts. The Metropolitan Career and Technical Center (aka the "Met") was the first BPL school, launched in 1996 as part of the Providence, Rhode Island public school system. Although each BPL school is unique, all adhere to the founding principles of: (a) individual learning plans, (b) authentic assessment, and (c) personalized curricula that combine active membership in a community, relevant problem-solving, and holistic student development.

New Country School

Personalized curricula are also illustrated by a grades 6–12 charter school in Henderson, Minnesota, called New Country (Wolk, 2010). Its size? 106 students and 21 staff. The portion of its curriculum that would be considered conventional is limited to a daily math block, a reading hour, and a painting class with an artist-in-residence. Beyond that, students spend more than half of each day on self-designed projects that involve learning across disciplines.

More specifically, each student develops and submits a project proposal and rationale for faculty approval.

> The proposal describes in detail what the student wants to learn, how he or she plans to do so, and how the project intersects with state standards. The student has to justify his or her project as a legitimate learning experience, show its value to the community, and estimate how many credits it is worth. Students keep a daily log of how they spend their time. Like Met students, New Country students work with community experts who evaluate them on their performance. Students also evaluate themselves, using a performance rubric to rate their work in three areas: critical thinking, leadership and innovation, and their performance on specific projects. (Wolk, 2010, p. 5)

How do New Country School structures support this version of personalized education? Each student has a computer and spends most of every day at a work station in a large, office-like atrium. Also available for student use are "a science room with lab equipment, an art studio, a greenhouse, a wood shop, mechanics/metal shop, and a conference room" (Wolk, 2010, p. 5). Students can work solo, in peer groups, or one-on-one with their advisors.

In both the New Country and BPL examples, boundaries between school and community are fluid. The curriculum is project-based, inquiry-oriented, and student-centered. Subject matter content and skills are engaged as needed. Instead of secondary school environments structured around self-contained classrooms and separate disciplines and departments, learning opportunities are individualized. Students are afforded a high degree of autonomy in creating their own learning plans. Expectations are similarly high for student self-regulation and demonstration of learning. Importantly, both overall school size and student–staff ratios are small enough to support strong interpersonal relationships, personalized curricula, and whole-person development.

What about quantifiable outcomes? Wolk (2010) reports that 75 percent of New Country School graduates go on to postsecondary education, and 25 percent take college courses *during* their high school years. According to BPL's website, 92 percent of its students graduate and 95 percent are accepted into college, compared to national averages of 52 percent and 45 percent, respectively (Big Picture Learning, n.d.). Castleman and Littky (2007) found that, over a ten-year period, the Met had a 94 percent daily attendance rate and a 95 percent graduation rate, compared to Providence City School averages of 80 percent and 55 percent, respectively.

From Whole-Child to Whole-School

In chapter 5, we discussed the usefulness of well-chosen themes around which to integrate varied subject matter content so as to make students' experience of the curriculum more holistic and meaningful. Some schools have expanded the concept of theme-based *units* and *projects* to theme-based curricula *writ large*.

For example, many urban districts offer theme-based *magnet* or *choice* schools, some started as part of decades-old initiatives to desegregate public schools racially by attracting diverse students across neighborhood boundaries. School-wide curricular emphases and concomitant efforts to draw students with particular talents or interests can show up as options such as "Integrated Technology in Arts and Sciences" schools in San Jose, California, or in school names like Culinary Arts Academy and Latino Studies at

Burns School, in Hartford, Connecticut. Charter schools also often employ school-wide themes as curriculum organizers and specializations.

Sometimes, such whole-school strategies incorporate both whole-child *personalization* (as described earlier) and theme-based school *culture* change. In terms of key concepts summarized in chapter 1, cultural transformation involves purposefully harmonizing the taught, the supported, the unwritten, and the experienced curricula around a particular set of values or principles. The following example of a theme-based curriculum that addresses content and culture, whole-child and whole-school, is drawn from Covey (2009). We present this illustration as another student-centered alternative to primarily standards-driven curricula.

A. B. Combs Elementary School

This magnet school in the Wake County Public School System in Raleigh, North Carolina, is organized around the theme of leadership, as originally expressed in Stephen Covey's influential book, *The Seven Habits of Highly Effective People* (1989) and since adapted to children and youth.

A. B. Combs is a K-5 school with approximately 800 students. Its holistic curricular approaches underscore children's physical health, social development, and character building, along with academic knowledge and skills. Combs emphasizes empowering students to take responsibility for their own learning and for the well-being of the whole school.

Similar to the examples of personalized curricula described earlier, A. B. Combs students identify unique academic and personal goals, and are responsible for tracking their own progress throughout the year. This individualized goal-setting and self-regulating preparation is the focus of the first week of every school year. It accompanies simultaneously revisiting the 7 Habits, developing student-generated classroom codes of cooperation and class mission statements, and creating art to decorate classrooms and the school's common areas. The children also "create, apply for, and interview for class leadership roles such as library leader, mail room leader, or classroom greeter" (Covey, 2009, p. 62).

Classroom greeters share with teachers the school-wide custom of welcoming each child by name, at the door of every classroom, every morning. While all children are taught to establish eye contact, greet, and welcome school visitors, teachers and classroom greeters often also shake each classmate's hand and articulate something positive about a recent accomplishment. This recurring adult and peer attention to personalization is aimed at nurturing a school culture wherein students know each other well, feel connected, and recognize different individual strengths.

Such culture-building helps to diminish conflict and classroom management problems. Teachers are also trained to capitalize on the disciplinary issues that do emerge as

> opportunities for student growth and self-regulation. For example, when conflicts arise between students, teachers may ask them to take a few moments to proactively control their emotions, seek first to understand, and come up with a win-win solution. Many times students do this on their own. (Covey, 2009, p. 63)

With widely-shared student responsibility for sustaining positive learning environments, teachers can concentrate on creating and sharing ideas for infusing the 7 Habits leadership principles into the taught curriculum. Covey (2009) offers several specific examples:

> When teaching a history lesson, a teacher might ask students how the historical figure they are studying could have handled things more proactively. Another teacher might use a science lesson to point out how Einstein synergized with his peers to get through school. Writing assignments may include writing a personal mission statement or discussing why it is important, when writing a poem or short story, to begin with the end in mind. Such forms of imagination also show up in clever hall displays, class activities, and student leadership roles. (Covey, 2009, p. 64)

As in the earlier Big Picture Learning and New Country School illustrations, A. B. Combs also extends its curricula beyond school walls. For example, each grade level comes together to implement at least one community service project every year. In the past, these have been the sort appropriate for elementary children, including leading canned food drives and helping the local chapter of the Red Cross.

Although too numerous to recount here, many other learning activities, special events, traditions, and community partnerships characterize A. B. Combs' leadership-themed curriculum and culture. For example, one particularly unusual leadership role for these young students is their participation in interviewing new teacher applicants. "Applicants are often stunned by the depth of students' questions" (Covey, 2009, p. 62). Routinely, students' ideas and contributions to the school are valued.

What kinds of results have been reported for this whole-child, whole-school effort to prioritize the learning of leadership in curriculum content and school culture? Over approximately ten years, enrollment rose from 350 to some 800, with a waiting list of interested students. Combs' parents report marked increases in students' self-confidence. Teachers note decreased discipline problems. Students' end-of-grade test performance rose from pass rates of 67% to 97%. The school is regularly visited by other educators, to learn from its successes. "More than 40 schools in the U.S. have now embedded the 7 habits into their schools' culture, and about 100 have begun the process this year" (Covey, 2009, p. 63).

From Whole-School to Broader Social Impact

So far in this chapter, we have illustrated two kinds of alternatives aimed at nurturing students holistically and diminishing the downsides of standardized, one-size-fits-all curricula. The first alternative centered on strategies to increase curriculum personalization. The other meshed personalization with a whole-school thematic curriculum (i.e., every child a leader). Each involved classroom-community boundary-spanning, defining part of students' holistic development as active participation in social contexts beyond the school's walls.

A third alternative extends the first two even further. Its aim is not only students' *personal* transformations, but broader *social* change as well. This approach emphasizes education's potential to re-shape the world around us (Apple & Beane, 2007). It moves beyond curriculum expectations for student *participation* in the local community, to *active citizenship* to improve the quality of community life. Its definition of a well-rounded student citizen includes questioning the status quo, thinking critically, collective problem-solving for community development, and addressing social injustices.

Apple and Beane (2007) refer to this curriculum alternative as *democratic* schooling, in part because one of the purposes of education in a democracy is societal—as well as individual—benefit. We turn next to a specific example of what such a curriculum can look like in practice.

Byrd Community Academy

Schultz (2007) recounts his firsthand experience as a teacher who co-constructed a democratic educational curriculum with his fifth-grade students over the course of the 2003–2004 academic year. It started with his desire to make school more meaningful and engaging for his mostly African American students from the infamous low-income Cabrini Green housing projects in the Chicago public school system.

Applying the transdisciplinary integration strategies discussed previously, Schultz began with students brainstorming problems affecting them and their community. There were no shortages of issues identified—a total of 89 problems surfaced in about an hour of class time. Some were broad social concerns for reducing homelessness or gang activity and cleaning up the local park. Most, however, centered on the dilapidated conditions of their own elementary school, Richard E. Byrd Community Academy: "no gym, no lunchroom, or auditorium; broken windows with bullet holes; no heat in the classroom; and leaky sinks, broken toilets, and no soap or paper towels in the bathrooms" (Schultz, 2007, p. 68). Students noticed the pattern in their lengthy listing and, at the teacher's suggestion, together developed an "action plan" for getting a new school built.

The proposed goal of a new school had been a community issue for years. In fact, students were reminded of it every day, not only by the school's long-neglected facilities but because there was a clearly visible sign on the fence of an adjacent property: "Site of the Future Byrd Elementary." The sign was some six years old, hung around the time the city and board of education promised the new building. Additionally, "the architectural plans depicting the new school design were on display in the lobby of our current dilapidated building" (Schultz, 2007, p. 72).

Schultz shared his fifth-graders' excitement about the class project's authenticity and importance. Nonetheless, he was also candid about his discomfort with the many unknowns that accompany student-generated, emergent (rather than preplanned) curricula aimed at living democratic ideals. He reflects:

> This was dangerous territory for me. For the first time as a teacher, I was on an equal level to my students: neither of us knew the potential outcome of our foray into the politics of the schools. . . . I wanted the new school as much as my students, but just like them, I did not know how to make this goal a reality. The students were no longer trying to solve contrived textbook questions. Instead it was an authentic quest with real components, challenges, and obstacles. (2007, p. 70)

Schultz decided to allow students to individually select action plan items of interest to them. The plan provided a general outline of the projected work, and interest groups intermittently shared their progress with the whole class. The patterns of action items that emerged from additional student brainstorming included "people we can talk to," "getting in newspapers and magazines," "putting pressure on people," and researching the history of the school.

Schultz (2007, p. 73) explains that the "people we can talk to" group, for example, set about interviewing school staff and administrators, leaders in area politics, members of the board of education, and several of Byrd Academy's corporate friends. The "ways to put pressure on" group worked on surveying kids, teachers, and staff; developing petitions; interviewing people with power in the community; writing letters to the legislature; inviting politicians to the school; holding a press conference; and producing a documentary video.

Together, the fifth-graders photographed school conditions, wrote extensively, and created graphs, charts, and a website to document Byrd's rundown facilities, to bring them to the attention of real-world audiences, and to record their project's trajectory. (See *www.projectcitizen405.com*). The students' action plan guided the curriculum. Their perseverance, research, and collaborative work succeeded in garnering widespread recognition and publicity.

Although a new Byrd school was never built, "Issues that the school engineer had been asking to have fixed for years finally received the attention they deserved. Lights, sidewalks, and drinking fountains were replaced, doors were fixed, windows were ordered, and even soap dispensers were installed in the bathrooms!" (Schultz, 2007, p. 78). More importantly, students were motivated by a democratically generated curriculum, learned a great deal, and experienced active citizenship. As their teacher observes:

> The students became so involved in the daily work of the project, they often came to school early, stayed late, and even showed up on their days off (p. 76) . . . . Over the course of the school year's integrated curriculum, standardized test scores of most students increased over the previous year without direct time spent on skill-and-drill test preparation that is so common in many urban schools. The students' attendance was an unprecedented 98 percent and there were rarely discipline issues. . . . Instead of succumbing to memorization and rote learning, the students naturally met standards of excellence since it was a necessity to solve the authentic problem (p. 78) . . . . In fact, their efforts went well beyond any standards or prescriptions, because they wanted and needed to learn the skills necessary in order to actively participate in their project. (p. 79)

Implications for School Leaders

In the four examples elaborated in this chapter, teacher and principal leadership were mutually reinforcing and critical to the alternative's success (Gupton, 2010).

Support Risk-Taking

A factor common to each of these illustrations is taking a chance to try something new or different from typical standards-driven curriculum and uniform assessments. At Byrd Community School, Schultz (2007) describes his principal as "extremely supportive" of his own and his fifth-grade students' risk-taking and political assertiveness. In the A. B. Combs example, Covey (2009) portrays the sense of urgency with which principal Muriel Summers rallied teachers, students, and community to build an integrated leadership curriculum and culture. And at the Big Picture Learning and New Country schools, it took risk-tolerant teachers and leaders to welcome students designing their own curricula and to trust personalization as a productive pathway to learning (Wolk, 2010).

Punitive state policies and media attention can contribute to relentless focus on standardized test scores. Similarly, state curriculum standards can lead to feelings that educators' hands are tied when it comes to developing nontraditional programs or creating alternative school structures. Yet, as this chapter has illustrated, counter-examples to standardized curricula and assessment practices exist throughout the United States and, according to Apple and Beane (2007) always have. (See box 6.1 for web resources on additional alternatives.)

Interestingly, Levin (2006) investigated decades of data from California, where school districts were allowed to apply for waivers from state regulations or educational policies they felt hindered their school improvement efforts. His research found that administrators and school boards frequently thought state policies were more restrictive than they actually were and that "the vast majority of all requests for waivers were unnecessary" (p. 173).

Hence, key takeaways for current and prospective school leaders: Don't let undue timidity about questioning commonplace practice prevent you or your teachers from upending familiar curriculum and assessment routines. As importantly, avoid regarding the familiar as "inevitable and immutable" (Hess, 2009, p. 30).

Welcome Divergent Thinking

Since the 1980s, expectations for shared decision-making have characterized U.S. public education. Building-based teams of teachers, administrators and, sometimes, parent and staff representatives have become institutionalized in schools (Wirt & Kirst, 2005). As discussed in chapter 2, norms of consensus-seeking and collegial leadership have numerous benefits, including collective responsibility for and ownership of shared goals.

BOX 6.1. WEB RESOURCES FOR ADDITIONAL ALTERNATIVES

Note: URLs can change unexpectedly.

Alternative Education Resource Organization (AERO)
http://www.educationrevolution.org/

Coalition of Essential Schools (CES)
http://www.essentialschools.org/

International Democratic Education Network (IDEN)
http://www.idenetwork.org/index.htm

The International Association for Learning Alternatives (IALA)
http://www.learningalternatives.net/

National Coalition of Alternative Community Schools (NCACS)
http://ncacs.org/ncacs.htm

Richard E. Byrd Community Academy, Chicago, IL
http://www.projectcitizen405.com/

However, cultures of collegiality and consensus can also result in painting-inside-the-lines mindsets and practices (Hess, 2009). Welcoming divergent thinking can offset these and other downsides of group-think. Some ways for principals to do so are to construct curriculum committees with diverse membership and to hire career-changers and others who come to teaching through nontraditional routes. As Hess points out, those

> who are not education careerists . . . are less likely to accept prevailing norms and more likely to ask, Why do we do it this way? The point is not that we should prefer nontraditional leaders to seasoned educators, but that standard practice can prevent decision makers from tapping into unconventional skills, insights, or ways of thinking. (p. 32)

Clearly, Muriel Summers modeled divergent thinking as school principal of A. B. Combs elementary magnet school. Administrators Dennis Littky and

Elliott Washor were divergent thinkers when they founded the first Big Picture Learning School. Yet, positional school leaders were not the only ones initiating curriculum improvements in this chapter's illustrations.

Provide Cover

In the example of Byrd Academy, teacher Brian Schultz was a divergent thinker about the fifth-grade curriculum and his students. Administrative leaders are needed who encourage and support teachers' creativity, unconventional instruction, and revamped routines. We discussed one aspect of such support in terms of principals "paving the way with school publics" in chapter 5.

Another important aspect entails backing the movement of innovative teachers and grassroots programming upward—that is, vertically through central office hierarchies and school boards. Hess (2009) refers to this element of leadership as "providing cover." By this, he means garnering support from above, as well as standing behind and defending teachers' risk-taking.

In the vernacular, providing cover may be understood as principals not letting innovative teachers hang out on limb alone when controversy arises or the going gets tough for curriculum change. It also means encouraging and facilitating school improvement initiatives, "even if some of them don't pan out," and accepting reversals of decisions without allowing these or other inevitable setbacks to deter future innovation (Hess, 2009, p. 32). Some turbulence must be anticipated and absorbed by principals who foster curriculum changes that differ significantly from typical practice.

A Final Thought

Curriculum improvement strategies for coordinating collective efforts to enhance children's basic skills are perennially important parts of educational leadership. Another significant role is guarding against excessive standardization and cookie-cutter approaches to curriculum content and instruction. Why? Because the latter do not work for all children, nor for all socially valued expectations of schools.

Taken together, illustrations of alternatives provide hopeful images for those seeking options to narrowed, basics-oriented curricula that can over-rely on standardized testing or neglect whole-child development. Next, we overview broader educational philosophies that help situate the question underlying these illustrations. That is, what kind of education do we want for our children?

7

~

Why Do Philosophy and Political Leadership Matter?

It's now your fourth year as principal. In the previous three, your introductory remarks for Curriculum Night have mostly been about helping parents understand their child's class schedule, so they could follow it and become acquainted with a variety of teachers. This year, you're planning a meatier introduction. You expect to share examples of curriculum improvements the school has been working on. You'll also overview programming initiated to address the student population's changing demographics and needs.

Are the curriculum accomplishments you're most proud of likely to resonate with parents and caregivers in attendance? How can you anticipate the kinds of questions or concerns audience members might have? To what extent are your values and aspirations for the school shared by others in the community?

Understanding fundamental variations among educational philosophies can facilitate school leaders' stock-taking of their environments. Additional leadership and political tools can also help. These philosophical and political considerations expand upon ideas introduced in chapter 1 as the school curriculum's social context (revisit figures 1.3 and 1.4).

The Curriculum Environment

Two issues contested throughout the history of K–12 public education in the United States are: What is the primary purpose of schooling? And, more concretely, What should the curriculum emphasize? (Pinar, Reynolds, Slattery, & Taubman, 2006). To summarize the varied responses to these questions that have recurred over time, four broad categories of thought are commonly identified: intellectual traditionalist, experientialist, social behaviorist, and reconstructionist (Kliebard, 1982; McNeil, 2003). Sometimes these categories are referred to as philosophies of education or conceptual frameworks; other times as perspectives, curriculum orientations, paradigms, theories, or schools of thought.

Regardless of label, the fundamental idea is that each reflects different ideals, aspirations, and worldviews that have created or reshaped curricula in the past, and that continue to contend for influence in local schools and districts (Marshall, Sears, & Schubert, 2000). To start this chapter, we overview key values and goals encompassed by each of these four perspectives on what a "good" curriculum is (see table 7.1).

Intellectual Traditionalist

Liberal arts traditions and education in the classics are often parts of what intellectual traditionalists would emphasize in their preferred school curricula (Beyer & Apple, 1998). The former generally values grounding in a variety of longstanding disciplines, such as history, literature, geography, the sciences, civics, mathematics, and the arts (Ravitch, 2010). The latter may include subjects such as logic, philosophy, and Latin. In both, learning for its own sake and for development of the mind is central (Posner, 2003). Transmitting enduring bodies of knowledge is considered key to intellectual growth and powers of reasoning.

The subject matter (discipline) itself is emphasized, in contrast to other frameworks that give priority to learners' needs and interests, or to the relationship of curriculum content to social context or times (Sowell, 2000). Intellectual traditionalists put their faith in studying the classics of literature and what they regard as "the finest in the Western cultural heritage" (Kliebard, 1982, p. 23).

Such emphases are invariably criticized for perpetuating elitist, culturally biased, adult-centered, expert-driven, or top-down approaches to what a good curriculum should be. However, proponents of this perspective view preservation, guardianship, and transmission of venerable traditions to next generations as essential purposes of education.

Manifestations of intellectual traditionalist curricula include back-to-basics educational movements and "great books" studies. William J. Bennett, U.S. secretary of education during the Reagan administration, advocated curricular traditionalism as a means to refocus and improve K–12 schooling.

"Core knowledge" curricula are contemporary examples of this school of thought (Hirsch, 1987, 2001).

Other terms you may see associated with or substituted for intellectual traditionalism include humanism, academic rationalism, and selected aspects of the educational philosophies sometimes referred to as perennialism or essentialism.

Experientialist

In part as a response to intellectual traditionalists' emphases on subject matter, experientialists advocate making *students* central to schooling. In the current vernacular, this approach to curricula can be considered emergent from the bottom up, learner-centered, or whole-child oriented.

The focus is on child development and helping individual learners grow to their fullest potential (Beyer & Apple, 1998). Healthy personal development and self-actualization are viewed as important purposes of education, in contrast to exclusive foci on academic development or the preservation of insights from "great" works. What students *experience* in schools is valued more highly than passing on predetermined or static bodies of knowledge (Marshall et al., 2000).

Capitalizing on learners' interests, as well as students' and teachers' active co-construction of curricular directions, are often features of experientialist orientations to schooling (Sleeter, 2005). Related approaches include problem-based, project-oriented, student self-directed, and discovery learning.

Common experientialist themes are curriculum flexibility and goals of inspiring intrinsic motivation, love of learning, imagination, improvisation, and "productive idiosyncrasy" (Eisner, 2001, p. 368). In the previous chapter, the personalized curricula of big-picture learning and New Country School illustrate experientialist philosophy in practice. The teacher-and-student co-created curriculum in Byrd Academy's fifth grade also embodies many of this perspective's key features.

These examples of experientialist ideals contrast vividly with the constancy valued by intellectual traditionalists. Whereas the latter assume that enduring disciplines best support well-grounded intellects, experientialists emphasize faith in students' abilities to imagine and address significant subject matter through integrated processes of learning how to learn.

"Progressive" education and "developmentalist" are terms typically associated with experientialist curricula. John Dewey (1938) may be the most quoted advocate of building on children's experiences and interests for more participative approaches to education. Contemporary manifestations of this curricular perspective can be found in varied kinds of alternative programs (see chapter 6) and in Montessori or other independent schools.

Perhaps needless to say, today's standards-based education reform policies—including the federal No Child Left Behind (NCLB) Act—do not constitute a particularly conducive environment for experientialist curricula (Sleeter, 2005). Instead, the current policy context is grounded in social behaviorism, the philosophy we elaborate next. Since this perspective has dominated K–12 practice in the recent past, we begin our overview by briefly recapping its historical roots.

Social Behaviorist

The industrialization of the U.S. economy during the early 1900s was accompanied by ever-growing faith in a set of beliefs made popular by Frederick Taylor, a mechanical engineer and management consultant (Spring, 2005). Taylorism (also known as *scientific management*) was largely grounded in ideas that contributed to productivity in factories: specialization of roles, precise timing and organization, the assembly of disparate pieces into a valued whole, linear progression, and frequent measurement of inputs, performance, and outcomes (Tyack, 1974). Increasing reliance on standardized procedures, testing, and measurement was further reinforced in that era by Edward Thorndike, a scholar considered the father of educational psychology (Marshall et al., 2000).

Together, these and other developments in academe and society engendered what is termed a *social efficiency* perspective or a *social behaviorist* orientation to curriculum. Among this perspective's core values are technical efficiency and the application of practices from business and industry to education and schools (Kliebard, 1982). These values manifest themselves in educational routines such as ability grouping and the organization of schools into grade levels, as well as movements such as results-focused standardization and outcomes-based education.

For example, applied to curriculum, efficiencies are sought through the specification of learning standards and outcome goals; curriculum mapping and sequencing; alignment among curriculum, instruction, and assessment; frequent student testing; systems of rewards and punishment to shape behavior; and the use of rubrics to evaluate learners' products (Sleeter, 2005).

Our chapters 2–4 detailed curriculum leadership approaches compatible with social efficiency perspectives. These and similar initiatives are aimed at tightly delimiting and coordinating teachers' and students' work, standardizing practice, capitalizing on time and resources, and producing uniform outcomes (Spring, 2005; Tyack, 1974).

Table 7.1. Simplified Overview of Four Curriculum Philosophies

Educational Philosophy	Curriculum Emphases	Priority Values	Example	Critiques
Intellectual Traditionalist	Subject matter; liberal arts disciplines	Transmission and preservation of enduring knowledge-base	"Great books" studies; core knowledge curricula	Perpetuates elitism; is adult-driven and culturally insensitive
Experientialist	Students' interests; individual needs	Self-actualization; whole-child development	Project-based learning; student–teacher co-created curricula	Lacks constancy; is difficult to coordinate and assess learning
Social Behaviorist	Standardization; social and workforce needs	Efficiency; utility for extant society	Today's standards-driven curricula and testing by grade levels	Reifies easiest-to-measure outcomes; narrows the curriculum
Reconstructionist	Critical thinking; challenging the status quo	Transformation of society; mobilization for increased equity	Students' collective action for community change	Fosters radicalism; lacks support outside academia

The influence of technical efficiency distinguishes the social behaviorist orientation to curricula in another way as well (Sowell, 2000). Whereas, in broadest terms, intellectual traditionalists emphasize *subject matter* and experientialists make *students* central to the curriculum, serving *society's interests* is fundamental to the social behaviorist perspective. (Hence the "social" part of its label.)

Accordingly, the purpose of schooling shifts to more utilitarian societal needs. For example: How well are school graduates prepared for the workforce? What gaps exist between the traits, skills, and behaviors of productive or successful adults, and those of children (Marshall et al., 2000)? The educational system is expected to address these gaps, in service to broader social, culturally valued, and economic ends.

Partially for this reason, social behaviorism is sometimes faulted for being an adult-centered, expert-driven, top-down approach to curricula (McNeil, 2003). In more pointed terms, Eisner (2001) critiques such technical-rational approaches for narrowing the curriculum, reducing educational experience to the pursuit of test scores, draining teachers' and children's creativity and imagination, marginalizing students' individual curiosities, and over-emphasizing "extrinsically defined attainment targets" that are easiest to measure (p. 369).

Reconstructionist

Concern for the social world beyond schools is also central to the reconstructionist perspective, although in ways significantly different from those of social behaviorists. Reconstructionists continually question the status quo and value education as a means of transforming (that is, reconstructing) society.

The aim is to create more inclusive and equitable social conditions for all, rather than to prepare graduates to fit into an existing work-world, politics, culture, and economy characterized by unfairness and disparity between haves and have-nots (Hewitt, 2006). Brian Schultz's fifth-graders' work to press local policy-makers to fulfill their promise of a new school building for their long-neglected community illustrated several of these aims (see chapter 6, Byrd Community School).

Reconstructionist curricula seek to equip learners with tools to critique and challenge longstanding power inequities, create more just societies, eradicate poverty, and empower groups that have been historically marginalized, subordinated, or disenfranchised (Apple, 1979; Freire, 1970). As such, this school of thought shares with experientialism a kind of grassroots, bottom-up orientation to both learners' roles within the curriculum and the purposes of education. Unlike the experientialist focus on individual self-actualization, however, reconstructionism emphasizes collective action to right group and broader social wrongs. (Note: You may also see the term *social meliorist* used instead of reconstructionist.)

Other contemporary manifestations of reconstructionist curricula include antiracism education, critical pedagogy, culturally responsive content and, more generally, the explicit study of social inequities in order to inform initiatives to upend them (Sleeter, 2005). However, in comparison to the historic ebbs and flows of influence that the other three perspectives have had on schooling in the United States, reconstructionism has yet to significantly shape either K–12 schools or curricula more generally (Spring, 2005). This may not be surprising, given that radical social change is the reconstructionist goal.

Taken Together

The ideas and examples synthesized so far in this chapter illustrate varied emphases among recurrent curriculum leadership concerns for *subject matter*, *students*, and *society's interests* (Marshall et al., 2000; Pinar et al., 2006). They also capture different ways of conceptualizing the main purposes of schooling, educators' roles, and the criteria against which the quality of a curriculum might be assessed (Zinn, 1996).

In the everyday world of K–12 schools, of course, teachers, administrators, and community constituents do not articulate their values or belief systems using the terms distinguished in this chapter. Nevertheless, underlying philosophies—even when unstated or unexamined—shape educators' priorities, community expectations, school cultures, and curricula. If leaders observe and listen carefully for the rationale behind particular curriculum decisions, demands, or conflicts, approximations of these four tacitly held perspectives emerge.

These distinctive frameworks may also be revealed by what is *absent* from school programs. Thus, the flip side of the question, "What is it we will focus our time and resources on?" becomes, "When we have to let something go in the school program, what should it be?" (Hewitt, 2006). Therefore noticing what has *gone by the wayside* in your school or district can also lead to insights about predominant curriculum philosophies.

In sum, the purpose of developing ideas and language for talking about distinct perspectives is not to "label" as an academic exercise, nor to rank one perspective as superior to another (Zinn, 1996, p. 108). Rather, it is to deepen school leaders' understanding of the dynamic forces that have and will likely continue to influence curriculum decision-making.

Political Ideologies

Of course, differences in educational philosophies are not the only source of potential contention regarding what gets taught and where scarce curriculum resources should be focused. Political ideology also comes into play.

Accordingly, school curriculum priorities need to take into account—and be responsive to—local and statewide political leanings. Questions to consider include, for example: Do primarily liberal constituencies characterize your school's context? Are politically conservative dynamics predominant?

Obviously, every locality includes a mix. And educational politics encompass continua of positions much more complex than that suggested by the liberal–conservative dualism. However, thinking in at least these terms can help curriculum leaders anticipate school community interests and concerns.

Moreover, sometimes helpful connections may be drawn between general political leanings and the curriculum philosophies elaborated earlier. For example, politically liberal constituencies may be more likely to support some of the progressive aims captured by experientialist or reconstructionist curricula. On the other hand, political conservativism could be expected to share greater affinity for intellectual traditionalist and social behaviorist curriculum approaches.

Interestingly, both congressional Democrats and Republicans supported the enactment of the most influential national policy currently shaping U.S. education, the NCLB Act of 2001. The parties originally did so for different reasons (Mehta, 2008; Wirt & Kirst, 2005).

Liberals were attracted by the continued federal funding that NCLB meant for schools, as well as the focus on closing persistent achievement gaps among student subgroups who differed by race, ethnicity, poverty, and other demographics. Conservatives were interested in reforming what they considered to be a failing educational system, as well as in reinforcing the idea of school choice for children attending schools deemed subpar. Liberals and conservatives alike rallied around NCLB's emphasis on standards and increased accountability for schools, both foci consistent with scientific management and social behaviorist curriculum principles.

So What?

Clearly, today's school leaders must be adept at functioning within a largely social behaviorist and standards-based education policy environment. At the same time, U.S. schools operate in a pluralistic democracy that honors disparate public opinion and values. Moreover, the adage remains true that "all politics are local." Therefore school leaders need to be knowledgeable about diverse perspectives—philosophical and political. Zinn (1996) underscores several benefits of doing so.

Self-Awareness

First, familiarity with different perspectives can lead to deeper self-knowledge, helping us clarify and name the predominant ways in which we think about our own leadership and curriculum priorities. Informed consciousness can inspire confidence in the foundations that guide our educational choices. It can also increase self-awareness of the mind's filters that selectively distort or tacitly blind us to other viewpoints and values.

Empathy

Second, since controversy over curricular matters often arises from differing expectations, understanding a range of perspectives can help us appreciate what may be driving others' actions or judgments. Appreciation can increase the chances that conflict might be replaced by respect, compromise, reconciliation of differences, mutual support, or coalition-building around other common interests. Teams, committees, the participation of varied constituents, and other working relationships can be more productive when the bases underlying reasoning are more widely understood. New insights can emerge from respectful dialog around differing political or philosophical ideals.

Policy Influence

A third benefit is that administrators and teachers are better prepared to shape, question, and challenge educational policy when they understand the varied value systems that motivate district, state, and federal directives impacting classroom and school practice (Fowler, 2004). This knowledge can inform proactive, collective advocacy for policies that support a particular school community's curriculum priorities. These understandings may also help avoid the pitfalls of uncritical acceptance of—or reactive stances to—perspectives that become taken-for-granted because of their ubiquity at particular points in time (Tyack, 1974).

Political Leadership Tools

As this chapter has emphasized, school curriculum improvement occurs within a broader sociopolitical context of diverse educational values and aspirations. Frequently, that context is also characterized by limited resources, multiple influential constituencies, and strong traditions of local school board governance and community involvement. For all of these reasons, four additional political skills are required to lead curriculum and other organizational improvement work (Bolman & Deal, 2003).

Communicating Direction

We introduced direction-setting in chapter 1 as one of three main ways that principals influence student learning. Chapters 2 and 3 followed-up with more specific strategies for focusing and coordinating curricula in order to advance collaboratively established school priorities. Chapter 4 elaborated features of research-based professional development practices that support teachers' collective efforts to sustain curricular and instructional direction.

Political insights complement this knowledge-base by underscoring constituencies *internal* and *external* to the school, as well as by recognizing conflict as differences in *interests* or *agenda* (Wirt & Kirst, 2005). In political terms, a school's direction is its agenda and, to succeed, it must address the interests of major constituencies.[1]

These realities require "knowing how others think and what they care about so that your agenda responds to their concerns" (Bolman & Deal, 2003, p. 205). Finely honed listening skills and regular opportunities to exchange ideas contribute to developing these sensitivities, complementing the empathy described above.

As part of information sharing and respectful exchange, savvy leaders also plant seeds: "leaving the kernel of an idea behind and letting it germinate and blossom so that it begins to float around the system from many sources other than the innovator" (Kanter, as cited in Bolman & Deal, 2003, p. 205). Seed-planting acknowledges that you, as an informed and thoughtful curriculum leader, bring your own ideals and advocacy to collaborative direction-setting.

The "elevator speech" is another tool for increasing awareness and exchange around your school's preferred curriculum improvement directions. This strategy, often promoted by community relations experts, is not a speech in the conventional sense of formal presentation. Instead, it means having at the tip-of-the-tongue a select few talking points that convey the key messages a leader wishes to advance (Conners, 2000; Kinder, 2000). For example, "We're so excited about the three benefits our new program will have for students . . . [then name them]." Or, "Our teachers are improving how they're helping English language learners by initiating X, Y, and Z in grades 4–6."

The elevator term is intended to highlight the importance of clarity and conciseness, since most elevator encounters are brief. It is also meant to suggest readiness to take advantage of routine or serendipitous communication opportunities that arise daily, inside and outside of schools.

Mapping the Political Terrain

Another political leadership skill involves systematically anticipating the environmental dynamics that could affect change initiatives, curricular or otherwise. Four steps to political mapping follow.

1. Become aware of the informal channels of communication that constituents pay attention to in and around your school (e.g., grapevines).
2. Identify persons and groups with political influence on the particular issue.
3. Determine possibilities for mobilizing both internal and external influentials.
4. Anticipate strategies that others are likely to employ (Pichault, as cited in Bolman & Deal, 2003, p. 207).

These four steps help clarify and anticipate: *who* would be most interested in a proposed change (either to thwart or help); *how much* clout each might bring to bear; and *what* each would potentially want or do. These preliminary analyses might suggest adaptations that could be made to original ideas, in order to garner more broad-based support.

Sound political maps also point to where realignment of current dynamics would need to occur, in order for a proposed initiative to move forward. That's where the next two strategies come in as well (Bolman & Deal, 2003).

Networking and Building Coalitions

"People skills" are essential to any leadership position. They include abilities to connect with others, to communicate effectively, and to cultivate positive relationships across differences and disagreement. Among these skills' strongest foundations are personal trustworthiness, competence, credibility, and integrity.

When the cultivation and expansion of positive relationships is undertaken for professional purposes, it is commonly referred to as *networking*. When networks are used to bring together groups of allies and influentials around proposed ideas, it is called *coalition building* or *political mobilization*.

This constellation of interpersonal, networking, and coalition-building leadership is often prerequisite to successful change, whether to a school's curriculum or other public institutions' undertakings. Whereas the political mapping described earlier helps to figure out whose support is required, durable relationships and networking increase the odds that allies will be there when leaders need them (Bolman & Deal, 2003).

Negotiating Differences

Ideally, worthy curriculum directions grounded in sound thinking will attract supporters on their merits. That is, *attraction* is preferable to attempting to *sell* curriculum improvement ideas.

However, as earlier syntheses demonstrated, disagreement about what makes a good curriculum is perennial, due to differing philosophical and political perspectives, or simply because there is seldom "one best way" of accomplishing educational goals. In their classic book, *Getting to Yes*, Fisher and Ury offer several ideas that can help school leaders reconcile differences using aptly named *win–win* approaches (as cited in Bolman & Deal, 2003, pp. 205–215):

1. **Separate the people from the problem.** Skillful reconciliation focuses on the substance of differences, steers clear of personal attacks, and maintains constructive interpersonal relationships with opponents. To help sustain equanimity and positive tone, remind yourself frequently that you will undoubtedly have to work with these same constituents again in the future.
2. **Focus on interests rather than positions.** In other words, if you lock onto a specific position (e.g., this particular alternative program is the only way to go), you unnecessarily narrow possibilities and can miss other ways to achieve a shared school goal (e.g., to better engage alienated students). Listen intently for, and ask open-ended questions to bring out, potential common interests.
3. **Create options.** Avoid homing in on the first possibility that surfaces, because doing so can prematurely shut off discussion and creative thinking about other options. Be willing to adapt your initial preferred solutions. Be responsive to constituents' ideas that advance agreed-upon directions through a different pathway than you may have originally had in mind. Leaders who are rigid or self-interested around one issue may find themselves with diminished credibility, networks, and coalitions for subsequent issues.

Understanding Advocacy

Two additional points are warranted regarding the political tools synthesized in this chapter.

First, political terrain-mapping and coalition-building focus attention on those who have power and influence in or around schools. The less privileged, minimally empowered, or politically naive may be rendered invisible in such approaches.

Therefore ethical school leadership also entails representing and advocating for those with scant political capital. The latter can include families living in poverty; students who've fallen through the cracks; constituents who, for a variety of legitimate reasons, don't show up at local PTO or school board meetings; newer teachers reluctant to voice opinions that counter those of administration or veteran teachers; those without "connections"; and other minority constituencies unique to particular schools.

Second, there's a considerable history of distaste for political strategies among educators, based on persistent myths that schools can or should be "above" politics (Wirt & Kirst, 2005). Referring to leaders and managers of all types of organizations, Bolman and Deal (2003) emphasize the relevance and practicality of political skills.

> The basic point is simple: as a manager, you need friends and allies to get things done. To get their support, you need to cultivate relationships. Hard-core rationalists and incurable romantics sometimes react with horror to such a scenario. Why should you have to play political games to get something accepted if it's the right thing to do? (p. 210) . . . . Like it or not, political dynamics are inevitable under conditions most managers face every day: ambiguity, diversity, and scarcity. (p. 211)

By situating school leadership within a dynamic sociopolitical context, light is shed on why reasonable people sometimes disagree on what makes a "good" curriculum and where scarce resources should be focused.

Note

1. Throughout this book, we intentionally use the term "constituency" rather than the more popular "stakeholder." To us, this choice better captures our overall themes of inclusive, facilitative leadership in public service to a school's various communities.

8

~

Wrapping Up

Visionary pragmatists recognize what is possible to accomplish in a specific context, but at the same time, see beyond that context. Visionary pragmatists reach for what may seem unattainable, seeking ways to turn the impossible into the possible. (Sleeter, 2005, pp. 181–182)

This brief quote captures several threads woven throughout this book. The first is that context matters. For this reason, leaders should be wary of claims touting *the* best way to facilitate curricular or instructional improvement of any sort. Community values, school size, faculty talents, district resources, state priorities and, most importantly, local students' needs and interests all have an impact on the kinds of leadership warranted for particular schools and moments in time. Accordingly, we have presented a variety of approaches for consideration and selective adaptation to local contexts.

Range of Leadership Strategies

Some of the practices described and illustrated in this book were what might be thought of as *technical* know-how. Examples included specific tools like curriculum maps, operational processes such as piloting materials prior to adoption, and suggestions for creating meeting agendas or protocols to increase the likelihood of productive curriculum workgroups. Staying up to date through reading and professional development networking are essential to continuously honing technical know-how. And an informed conceptual knowledge base—such as the fundamentals this book provides—can help leaders recognize how "the latest popular recipe" may relate to enduring big ideas in curriculum work.

Other strategies highlighted in this volume were more *political*. That is, they were grounded in the reality that what's included in or omitted from school curricula reflects differing values, power, and potential conflicts. Examples of political leadership included welcoming divergent perspectives, providing cover for teachers implementing nonstandardized curricula, and harnessing coalitions to smooth pathways toward change.

In contrast, yet another aspect of leadership emphasized could be understood as *cultural*. These more amorphous yet salient influences recognize that leaders play prominent roles in creating and sustaining local conditions for educational initiatives. These conditions, climate, or culture, are seldom neutral. Instead, they either help or hinder curricular and other improvement efforts. How much time principals devote to the instructional program, the degree to which they can be counted on for curriculum support, and the tone set through their actions and priorities, all shape the conditions in which curriculum improvement work occurs.

In addition to technical competencies, political savvy, and culture-building, *interpersonal* skills were also underscored throughout this volume. The personal, human side of leadership included examples of self-awareness, empathy, active listening, communication skills, role-modeling, and trust-building. Many of these competencies intersect with leaders' tone-setting influence on the overall school environment and culture. However interpersonal leadership is also distinguished by the unique one-to-one conversations and relationships school principals have with teachers, students, and community members. In short, school leaders' communication and human relations with others as individuals invariably create emotional wakes (Scott, 2009). These waves can propel advancement of, or churn resistance to curriculum initiatives.

Whether technical, political, cultural, or interpersonal, these and other leadership skills can be learned and continuously sharpened when raised to consciousness and practiced over time (Bolman & Deal, 2003). Our hope is that readers revisit this guidebook periodically, to refresh awareness of both:

- The importance of the school curriculum
- The multiple leadership approaches that can contribute to its improvement.

Range of Possibilities

A second thread woven through this text and captured by this chapter's opening quote entails seeing beyond current contexts. For this reason, we contrasted integrated models with subject-centered approaches to curriculum implementation. We compared today's predominantly social behaviorist and intellectually traditionalist philosophies of education to experientialist and reconstructionist visions. We described programs that were more personalized than standardized, to address the needs of students who may be unmotivated by or unsuccessful with conventionally organized curricula. We presented examples of alternatives to commonplace standards-centered school practices, including whole-child and whole-school–oriented program initiatives.

The curriculum alternatives illustrated set their sights on promoting well-rounded graduates while ameliorating the downsides of homogeneous and assessment-driven programming. All were examples from real schools operating within the most recent ten years. Each involved both bottom-up and top-down initiative and support.

These alternative possibilities tap into the *aspirational* side of leadership for student learning. They remind us that educational leaders are uniquely positioned to oversee the bigger picture of curricula that can cross grade-level and subject-area boundaries. That broader vantage point accentuates leaders' responsibilities to critically question the status quo, to stretch their own and others' thinking, to inspire creative problem-solving, and to nurture educational goals aimed beyond today's norms.

Enduring Tensions in Curriculum Leadership

On the one hand, the *visionary pragmatism* this book and Sleeter's quote encompass may seem an oxymoron. After all, doesn't pragmatism focus on getting things done in the near term? Aren't pragmatists' strengths their abilities to recognize and accomplish what works within current parameters of opportunities and constraints? In contrast, aren't visionaries' dreams unimpeded by prevailing thought? Don't their visions rouse us *because* they tap into imagination and ambitions that presently seem improbable?

Looked at another way, visionary pragmatism can be understood as but one of several paradoxes or tensions that characterize curriculum leadership. None of these tensions are new. All can be expected to continue into the future.

- **Consistency and flexibility.** For example, a perennial tension revolves around the relative benefits to students of tightly aligned curricula that consistently build from one concept or grade level to the next, versus less linear, more flexible content responsive to particular groups of students' interests or strengths.
- **Coordination and autonomy.** A related tension occurs between teachers' independent decision-making as professionals with particular expertise and administrative leaders' coordinating roles among multiple specialists.
- **Centralization and decentralization.** Similarly, tensions exist among governing authorities with interests in shaping school curricula: for example, national influences such as Common Core Standards, state-level assessments and guidance, and district policies and priorities.

In parts of the world where Ministries of Education are highly directive, where materials and texts are centrally prescribed by grade level and subject, or where life-changing national exams hold sway over students and teachers, the tensions summarized above may be nonissues.

However, strong U.S. traditions of local educational governance mean these challenges regularly affect curriculum decision-making. Visionary pragmatists accept ambiguities as givens in leadership work. They view tensions, conflict, and debate as potential sources of creativity and dynamic problem-solving. And they capitalize on the equally robust U.S. traditions of participatory democracy and teacher empowerment. That is, curriculum leaders do not grapple with these tensions alone.

This point underscores a third thread woven throughout this book: curriculum improvement grounded in dialog and collaboration among principals, teachers, and teacher leaders knowledgeable about particular students and school communities. This vision of shared curriculum leadership requires addressing practical matters of making *time* for collaboration. Although time was briefly discussed in chapter 2, it is so critical to curriculum improvement work that we conclude this volume by elaborating further.

Time to Collaborate

How have schools created more time for professional collaborations? Watts and Castle's (1993) comprehensive syntheses of five options remain relevant today. We draw primarily from that seminal work here, while updating with examples from more recent resources (e.g., Bowgren & Sever, 2010; Johnston, Knight, & Miller, 2007; Khorsheed, 2007; Lauer & Matthews, 2007;

Richardson, 2007; Sever & Bowgren, 2007; Tienken & Stonaker, 2007; White & McIntosh, 2007). Although overlap exists among the five options, we illustrate each separately to facilitate understanding.

Schedule Common Planning Time

One strategy for structuring within-school-day time for collaboration centers on synchronizing the preparation periods of grade-level, department, interdisciplinary, or other targeted groups of teachers. This approach is grounded in the premise that local school traditions or collectively bargained agreements allot specified amounts of teacher planning/preparation time without student contact each day or week.

At the secondary level, job-embedded common time for teacher workgroups may be built into the master schedule of course offerings. In elementary settings, such scheduling typically involves coordinating when children are *pulled out* of "regular" classrooms to participate in physical education, music, other arts, library, computer labs, or additional specialized curricula. In some instances, common planning periods can be extended by selectively connecting them to other noninstructional times (for example, recess or lunch periods every two weeks), if teachers or unions agree to such an option for creating more within-school opportunities for group efforts.

A variation of the common planning time model is used in the Papillion-La Vista, Nebraska public schools. That district fosters different ways of providing weekly professional collaboration time at its 16 component schools (Johnston et al., 2007). Some principals help extend teacher team meetings that start a half hour before students arrive by organizing literacy coaches or other staff to lead activities to begin the students' day. Sometimes multiple classes are combined for these beginning-of-day lessons and activities. In secondary schools that start with a homeroom session, some principals arrange for similar coverage, to free up selected teachers' time for collaborative work that amplifies before-school contracted time. This district's examples incorporate elements of a second approach summarized next.

Reduce Teachers' Contact Time with Students

A variety of methods have been used to release selected teachers from some instructional duties to carve out time for periodic collaboration during the workday while maintaining traditional school day start and dismissal times for students. Most involve enlisting other adults to substitute-teach classes or otherwise supervise children's learning activities during the time for which targeted collaborators are freed up from classroom instruction. Replacements may include existing paid or unpaid personnel such as teaching assistants, other support staff, college interns, administrators, community partners, volunteers, or members of teaching teams.

Sometimes, educational programming that can accommodate large groups of students with fewer adult supervisors can free up selected teachers' time. Examples include student assemblies of various kinds, theater performances, or special presentations by older students, business volunteers, or community groups.

Secondary schools with vocational internships, school-to-work apprenticeships, or community service expectations may be able to use students' off-site field experiences as opportunities for teacher collaboration time. For example, if such off-campus activities could be scheduled for the same hours or part-of-day each week, teachers' classroom instructional responsibilities might be eliminated for regular blocks of time.

Although the methods noted so far maintain children's usual school arrival and departure times, other options for freeing up collaboration time for all school personnel involve releasing students early or starting school late on designated days. For example, the Findlay City School District in Findlay, Ohio, used a two-hour delay in the start of classes to enable teachers to work together from 7:00 to 9:00 A.M. once each quarter (White & McIntosh, 2007, p. 32). Similarly, the Carman-Ainsworth Community Schools in Flint, Michigan, collectively bargained an agreement to start school an hour later than usual each Wednesday morning to free up time for teacher collaboration by grade level or subject area (Richardson, 2007). And in Loveland, Colorado, students are dismissed early each Wednesday where, by contract, "some of these afternoons are designated for teachers to work on their professional goals, others are for district-wide curriculum alignment, and the remaining are for site-based staff development" (Lauer & Matthews, 2007, p. 39). The Maine-Endwell School District in upstate New York dismisses students two or three hours early for teachers' professional collaboration on a differentiated schedule shared well in advance with parents: six times a year for its two elementary schools, four times for the middle school, and three times for the high school (Sever & Bowgren, 2007).

Early-release and late-start approaches are only appropriate for schools that already exceed minimum instructional hours/days mandated by different states. For those that do not, the following modification may be a better alternative.

Bank Teachers' Contact Time with Students

Banking minutes and hours is a strategy for creating blocks of time for teacher collaboration without diminishing students' total instructional time with their regular teachers in any given week. This approach can take varied forms. The commonality among them is that not every school day begins and ends at the same time. Sometimes, extended instructional time during four days of the week is "saved up" (deposited, in banking terms), so that it can be "expended" (i.e., withdrawn) on a fifth day, when students either arrive later or exit school earlier than the other four days. The deposited and withdrawn minutes leave the weekly balance of instructional time for students even.

For example, the Papillion-La Vista district in Nebraska considered feedback from teachers and found that adding ten minutes of daily instructional time fell within collectively bargained agreements (Johnston et al., 2007). By extending each school day in this way, they were able to bank time to create six professional collaboration days for teachers, spread across the school year.

Richardson (2002) shares the illustration of Addison Elementary School in Marietta, Georgia. There, the school day starts ten minutes earlier and ends ten minutes later than it had in the past, for four days a week. Those 80 minutes of banked instructional time were exchanged for releasing students from school at 1:30 p.m. on Wednesdays, so that teachers could work together each Wednesday afternoon. Some high schools follow similar banking models, but schedule later arrival times (rather than early release) for students on the fifth day.

Buy Additional Time

More expensive ways to create collaboration time involve hiring substitutes or other support staff to free up teacher time, as well as compensating regular teachers for hours dedicated beyond the contracted work day or year. Historically, for example, much curriculum development work has been accomplished during summer months, by paying stipends to teachers who volunteered, were selected by colleagues, or were tapped by administrators. Sometimes, weekends and breaks during the school year have been used for similar purposes, if sufficient numbers of teachers are willing to trade personal time for remuneration.

Bowgren and Sever (2010) offer a substitute roll-through model designed to minimize disruption to regular classroom instruction while enabling professional collaboration during the school day. This model requires hiring sufficient numbers of substitutes to cover one grade level, department, or other identified group of teachers at a time. The cohort of substitutes teaches for one or two hours while the specified grade-level, department, or other group of teachers works together. The first group of released teachers then returns to teach the rest of the day, while the substitute cohort "rolls" to the next set of classrooms. Thus, within just a few days (depending on school size), all teachers in a school can gain additional time to collaborate with other adults in their school.

Capitalize on Existing Time

When funding, substitutes, or other time-generating options are not available, using existing time wisely becomes even more important. That often entails organizing and focusing faculty, grade-level, and department meetings to be as productive and learning-centered as possible. It can also entail taking full advantage of the noninstructional work days included in teacher contracts.

For example, the public school district of Monroe Township, New Jersey, reorganized time for professional collaboration by shifting from two to one teacher preparation days immediately prior to opening day for students (Tienken & Stonaker, 2007). The second day without students was moved to a month later in the fall for additional adult learning and collaboration time. The district also timed several student early-release days throughout the year so as to meet state requirements for instructional days without adding work hours to teachers' contractual work days. The latter also contributed to more adult collaboration time. The Monroe Township example illustrates the idea of spreading teacher collaboration days across the calendar to provide more frequent, shorter school-based professional group work opportunities.

Khorsheed (2007) suggests rethinking student grouping as another means of freeing up small teams of teachers to work together during the regular school day. She shares an example at Garfield Elementary School in Livonia, Michigan. There, three first-grade classes of 20 students each were reorganized into two groups of 30 students for music and physical education, followed by recess. "In this way, three classes were covered by two specialist teachers, and three classroom teachers were able to collaborate for at least an hour" (p. 45).

Practical Pros and Cons

Of course, challenges and downsides accompany the benefit of increasing time for collaborative curriculum improvement work. Some entail financial costs, modifications to bus schedules, and irregular school start–dismissal times that may be confusing or inconvenient to parents and caregivers. Others involve treating specialty subject teachers (e.g., the arts, computer lab, physical education) differently than regular classroom teachers. Some result in decreased individual teacher planning time and increased teaching by substitute personnel. Many necessitate negotiations with unions or professional associations.

What are some steps leaders can take to generate support for changed staff or student time in school? Richardson's (2002) suggestions continue to be relevant today:

- Give teachers a strong voice in exploring options and planning any changes. Share with them the possibilities described earlier and the examples of actual schools that have implemented different strategies for making time. Invite them to brainstorm other possibilities that might work for your school. Involve teacher associations, unions, and collective bargaining leaders early in the process.
- Negotiate directly the trade-offs faculty, staff, and administrators are open to—and unwilling to touch—in order to gain time for professional collaborations.
- Involve parents and other community caregivers in discussions, particularly if your plans are likely to affect teacher contact time with children or alter school start and dismissal times. Be prepared with clear explanations of how your school's professional collaboration goals are tightly linked to student learning priorities. Provide examples of how students are likely to benefit from curriculum improvements.
- Pilot any new plans for at least a year prior to committing to them. When possible, piloting several different approaches within the same school district can produce valuable insights and comparisons of costs and benefits.

The Promise of Curriculum Leadership

We've covered considerable ground in this journey to understand and illustrate ways in which school leaders can facilitate and support curriculum improvement. On one hand, the ever-increasing emphasis on student learning outcomes puts additional pressure on all educational leaders, whether in classrooms or administrative offices. Nonetheless, the public commonly holds building principals accountable for overall school and program quality. These are weighty responsibilities.

On the other hand, the current press for leadership accountability also empowers principals to insist on priority setting and collective focus on what students learn. Such accountability can compel greater clarity and purposefulness in short- and long-term curriculum planning. It can help leaders cut through the clutter of other issues that invariably appear to be urgent but—through the filter of student learning priorities—may actually be less central. It can clarify resource and personnel decision-making, and provide powerful justification for how administrative and teacher leaders choose to concentrate their shared energies.

Taken together, the principal's roles elaborated in this guidebook represent key opportunities for *instructional leadership*. Although much has been written about this seemingly lofty term, we think of it simply as keeping the *educational* in educational administration. In short, it means keeping the school's collective work centered on enhancing student learning, and keeping administrative leadership focused on supporting children's learning through curriculum and school improvement.

For these reasons, we challenge conventional notions about how removed educational administration is from children and classrooms. This book's many examples of where, how, and why strong leaders intervene to impact education counter such misleading lore.

We conclude by reminding current principals of how important their everyday acts are to both students' and teachers' school experiences. And we hope this vision of curriculum leadership inspires veteran teachers and prospective administrators to consider the principalship as a career choice for themselves.

References

Abrams, L., & Madaus, G. (2003). The lessons of high-stakes testing. *Educational Leadership, 61*(3), 31–35.

Allen, J. (2007). *Creating welcoming schools: A practical guide to home-school partnerships with diverse families.* New York: Teachers College Press.

Anyon, J. (2005). *Radical possibilities.* New York: Routledge.

Apple, M. (1979). *Ideology and curriculum.* London: Routledge.

Apple, M., & Beane, J. (Eds.). (2007). *Democratic schools: Lessons in powerful education, 2nd ed.* Portsmouth, NH: Heinemann.

Au, W. (2007). High-stakes testing and curricular control: A qualitative metasynthesis. *Educational Researcher, 36*(5), 258–67.

Beane, J. (2002). Beyond self-interest: A democratic core curriculum. *Educational Leadership, 59*(7), 26–29.

Beane, J. (1997). *Curriculum integration: Designing the core of democratic education.* New York: Teachers College Press.

Beyer, L., & Apple, M. (Eds.). (1998). *The curriculum: Problems, politics, and possibilities.* Albany: State University of New York Press.

Big Picture Learning. (n.d.) Retrieved April 25, 2011, from http://www.bigpicture.org.

Birman, B., Desimone, L., Porter, A., & Garet, M. (2000). Designing professional development that works. *Educational Leadership, 57*(8), 28–33.

Blumberg, A., & Blumberg, P. (1994). *The unwritten curriculum: Things learned but not taught in schools.* Thousand Oaks, CA: Corwin.

Bolman, L., & Deal, T. (2003). *Reframing organizations: Artistry, choice, and leadership, 3rd ed.* San Francisco: Jossey-Bass.

Bowgren, L., & Sever, K. (2010). *Differentiated professional development in a professional learning community.* Bloomington, IN: Solution Tree Press.

Castleman, B., & Littky, D. (2007). Learning to love learning. *Educational Leadership*, 64(8), 58–61.

Conners, G. (2000). *Good news: How to get the best possible media coverage for your school*. Thousand Oaks, CA: Corwin.

Covey, S. (2009). A school for leadership. *Educational Leadership*, 67(2), 61–66.

Covey, S. (1989). *The seven habits of highly effective people*. New York: Simon & Schuster.

Darling-Hammond, L., Wei, R. C., Andree, A., Richardson, N., & Orphanos, S. (2009). *Professional learning in the learning profession: A status report on teacher development in the United States and abroad*. Dallas, TX: National Staff Development Council.

David, J. (2008). What the research says about pacing guides. *Educational Leadership*, 66(2), 87–88.

Desimone, L. (2009, April). Improving impact studies of teachers' professional development. *Educational Researcher*, 38, 181–99.

Dewey, J. (1938). *Experience and education*. New York: Macmillan.

Drake, S. (2007). *Creating standards-based interdisciplinary curricula*. Thousand Oaks, CA: Corwin.

DuFour, R. (2001). In the right context. *Journal of Staff Development*, 22(1), 14–17.

DuFour, R. (2002). One clear voice is needed in the din. *Journal of Staff Development*, 23(2), 60–61.

DuFour, R., Eaker, R., & Burnette, R. (2002). *Reculturing schools to become professional learning communities*. Bloomington, IN: National Education Service.

Eisner, E. (2001). What does it mean to say a school is doing well? *Phi Delta Kappan*, 82(5), 367–72.

English, F. (1980). Curriculum mapping. *Educational Leadership*, 37(7), 558–59.

English, F. (2010). *Deciding what to teach and test: Developing, aligning, and leading the curriculum* (3rd ed.). Thousand Oaks, CA: Corwin.

Erickson, H. L. (2007). *Concept-based curriculum and instruction for the thinking classroom*. Thousand Oaks, CA: Corwin.

Fowler, F. (2004). *Policy studies for educational leaders, 2nd ed.* Upper Saddle River, NJ: Pearson Education.

Freire, P. (1970). *Pedagogy of the oppressed*. New York: Seabury.

Fullan, M. (2007). *The new meaning of educational change, 4th ed.* New York: Teachers College Press.

Garet, M., Porter, A., Desimone, L., Birman, B., & Yoon, K. (2001). What makes professional development effective? Results from a national sample of teachers. *American Educational Research Journal*, 38(4), 915–45.

Glatthorn, A., Boschee, F., & Whitehead, B. (2006). *Curriculum leadership: Development and implementation*. Thousand Oaks, CA: Sage.

Glatthorn, A., & Jailall, J. (2009). *The principal as curriculum leader: Shaping what is taught and tested*. Thousand Oaks, CA: Corwin.

Glickman, C., Gordon, S., & Ross-Gordon, J. (2009). *The basic guide to supervision and instructional leadership* (2nd ed.). Boston: Pearson/Allyn & Bacon.

Gordon, S. (2004). *Professional development for school improvement.* Boston: Pearson/ Allyn & Bacon.

Greene, M. (1985). The role of education in democracy. *Educational Horizons, 63* (Special Issue), 3–9.

Gupton, S. (2010). *The instructional leadership toolbox: A handbook for improving practice* (2nd ed.). Thousand Oaks, CA: Corwin.

Hale, J. (2008). *A guide to curriculum mapping: Planning, implementing, and sustaining the process.* Thousand Oaks, CA: Corwin.

Hass, G. (1987). *Curriculum planning: A new approach* (5th ed.). Boston: Allyn & Bacon.

Herber, H. (1978). *Teaching reading in content areas* (2nd ed.). Englewood Cliffs, NJ: Prentice-Hall.

Hess, F. (2009). Cages of their own design. *Educational Leadership, 67*(2), 29–33.

Hewitt, T. (2006). Chapter 11: Managing and implementing the curriculum. In *Understanding and shaping the curriculum: What we teach and why* (pp. 287–314). Thousand Oaks, CA: Sage.

Hirsch, E. D. Jr. (1987). *Cultural literacy: What every American needs to know.* Boston: Houghton Mifflin.

Hirsch, E. D. Jr. (2001). Seeking breadth and depth in the curriculum. *Educational Leadership, 59*(2), 22–25.

House, J., & Taylor, R. (2003). Leverage on learning: Test scores, textbooks, and publishers. *Phi Delta Kappan, 84*(07), 537–41.

Jacobs, H. (Ed.) (2004). *Getting results with curriculum mapping.* Alexandria, VA: Association for Supervision and Curriculum Development (ASCD).

Jacobs, H. (Ed.). (1989). *Interdisciplinary curriculum: Design and implementation.* Alexandria, VA: Association for Supervision and Curriculum Development (ASCD).

Jacobs, H. (1997). *Mapping the big picture.* Alexandria, VA: Association for Supervision and Curriculum Development.

Johnston, J., Knight, M., & Miller, L. (2007). Finding time for teams. *Journal of Staff Development, 28*(2), 14–19.

Khorsheed, K. (2007). Four places to dig deeper to find more time for teacher collaboration. *Journal of Staff Development, 28*(2), 43–45.

Killion, J. (2002). *Assessing impact: Evaluating staff development.* Oxford, OH: National Staff Development Council.

Kinder, J. (2000). *A short guide to school public relations.* Bloomington, IN: Phi Delta Kappa Educational Foundation.

Kliebard, H. (1982). Education at the turn of the century: A crucible for curriculum change, *Educational Researcher, 11*(1), 16–24.

Langer, G., Colter, A., & Goff, L. (2003). *Collaborative analysis of student work: Improving teaching and learning.* Alexandria, VA: Association for Supervision and Curriculum Development.

Lauer, D., & Matthews, M. (2007). Teachers steer their own learning. *Journal of Staff Development, 28*(2), 36–41.

Leithwood, K., Louis, K. S., Anderson, S., & Wahlstrom, K. (2004). *Review of research: How leadership influences student learning*. New York: The Wallace Foundation. Retrieved June 29, 2009, from http://www.wallacefoundation.org/KnowledgeCenter/KnowledgeTopics/CurrentAreasofFocus/EducationLeadership/Pages/HowLeadershipInfluencesStudentLearning.aspx.

Leithwood, K., & Montgomery, D. (1986). *Improving principal effectiveness: The principal profile*. Toronto: Ontario Institute for Studies in Education Press.

Levin, H. (2006). Why is this so difficult? In F. Hess (Ed.), *Educational entrepreneurship: Realities, challenges, possibilities* (pp. 165–82). Cambridge, MA: Harvard Education Press.

Littky, D., & Grabelle, S. (2004). *The big picture: Education is everyone's business*. Alexandria, VA: Association for Supervision and Curriculum Development.

Little, C. (2001). What matters to students. *Educational Leadership, 59*(2), 61–64.

Marshall, J., Sears, J., & Schubert, W. (2000). *Turning points in curriculum*. Upper Saddle River, NJ: Merrill.

Marzano, R., Waters, T., & McNulty, B. (2005). *School leadership that works: From research to results*. Alexandria, VA: Association for Supervision and Curriculum Development.

McNeil, J. (2003). *Curriculum: The teacher's initiative, 3rd ed.* Upper Saddle River, NJ: Pearson Education.

McTighe, J., Seif, E., & Wiggins, G. (2004). You can teach for meaning. *Educational Leadership, 62*(1), 26–30.

McTighe, J., & Thomas, R. (2003). Backward design for forward action. *Educational Leadership, 60*(5), 52–55.

McTighe, J., & Wiggins, G. (2004). *Understanding by design professional development workbook*. Alexandria, VA: Association for Supervision and Curriculum Development.

Mehta, J. (2008). How did we get here? *Politics of Education Association Bulletin, 33*(1), 1–6.

Murphy, J., Elliott, S., Goldring, E., & Porter, A. (2006). *Learning-centered leadership: A conceptual foundation*. Wallace Foundation & the Learning Sciences Institute at Vanderbilt University. Retrieved June 24, 2009, from http://www.wallacefoundation.org/wallace/learning.pdf.

Newmann, F. (2010). Can depth replace coverage in the high school curriculum? In F. Parkay, G. Hass, & E. Anctil (Eds.), *Curriculum leadership readings for developing quality educational programs* (pp. 551–56). Boston: Allyn & Bacon.

Parkay, F., Hass, G., & Anctil, E. (2010). *Curriculum leadership: Readings for developing quality educational programs, 9th ed.* Boston: Allyn & Bacon.

Pinar, W., Reynolds, W., Slattery, P., & Taubman, P. (2006). *Understanding curriculum, 5th ed.* New York: Peter Lang Publishing.

Posner, G. (2003). *Analyzing the curriculum*. New York: McGraw-Hill.

Ravitch, D. (2010). In need of a renaissance. *American Educator, 34*(2), 10–22, 42.

Reeves, D. (2006). Chapter 17: Power standards: How leaders add value to state and national standards. In *The Jossey-Bass reader on educational leadership*, 2nd ed. (pp. 239–47). San Francisco: Jossey-Bass.

Rettig, M., McCullough, L., Santos, K., & Watson, C. (2003). A blueprint for increasing student achievement. *Educational Leadership*, 61(3), 71–76.

Rettig, M., McCullough, L., Santos, K., & Watson, C. (2004). *From rigorous standards to student achievement: A practical process*. Larchmont, NY: Eye On Education.

Richardson, J. (2001, February/March). Group wise: Strategies for examining student work together. *Tools for Schools Newsletter*, 1–6.

Richardson, J. (2002, August, September). Think outside the clock: Create time for professional learning. *Tools for Schools Newsletter*, 1–7.

Richardson, J. (2007). Bargaining time. *The Learning System* [NSDC newsletter], 2(6), pp. 1, 6.

Schultz, B. (2007). "Feelin' what they feelin": Democracy and curriculum at Cabrini Green. In M. Apple & J. Beane (Eds.), *Democratic schools: Lessons in powerful education*, 2nd ed. (pp. 62–82). Portsmouth, NH: Heinemann.

Scott, S. (2009). Take responsibility for your emotional wake. *Journal of Staff Development*, 30(4), 63–64.

Segall, A. (2004). Blurring the lines between content and pedagogy. *Social Education*, 68(7), 479–82.

Sergiovanni, T. (2006). *The principalship: A reflective practice perspective*, 5th ed. Boston: Pearson.

Sever, K., & Bowgren, K. (2007). Shaping the workday. *Journal of Staff Development*, 28(2), 20–23.

Sleeter, C. (2005). *Un-standardizing the curriculum: Multicultural teaching in the standards-based classroom*. New York: Teachers College Press.

Sowell, E. (2000). *Curriculum: An integrative introduction*, 2nd ed. Upper Saddle River, NJ: Merrill/Prentice Hall.

Spillane, J. (2006). *Distributed leadership*. San Francisco: Jossey-Bass.

Sprenger, M. (2003). *Differentiation through learning styles and memory*. Thousand Oaks, CA: Corwin.

Spring, J. (2005). *Conflict of interests: The politics of American education*, 5th ed. Boston: McGraw-Hill.

Strong, R., Silver, H., & Perini, M. (2001). Making students as important as standards. *Educational Leadership*, 59(3), 56–61.

Tallerico, M. (2005). *Supporting and sustaining teachers' professional development: A principal's guide*. Thousand Oaks, CA: Corwin.

Tienkin, C., & Stonaker, L. (2007). When every day is professional development day. *Journal of Staff Development*, 28(2), 24–29.

Tomlinson, C., & McTighe, J. (2006). What really matters in learning? Content. In *Integrating differentiated instruction and understanding by design* (pp. 24–37). Alexandria, VA: Association for Supervision and Curriculum Development.

Tyack, D. (1974). *The one best system*. Cambridge, MA: Harvard University Press.

Tyler, R. (1949). *Basic principles of curriculum and instruction*. Chicago: University of Chicago Press.

Ubdexchange.org Website affiliated with the Association for Supervision and Curriculum Development, to support the Understanding by Design (UbD) approach to curriculum development.

Udelofen, S. (2005). *Keys to curriculum mapping: Strategies and tools to make it work*. Thousand Oaks, CA: Corwin.

Von Zastrow, C., & Jance, H. (2004). *Academic atrophy: The condition of the liberal arts in America's public schools*. Washington, DC: Council for Basic Education.

Wahlstrom, K., Seashore Louis, K., Leithwood, K., & Anderson, S. (2010). *Investigating the links to improved student learning: Executive summary of research findings*. New York: The Wallace Foundation. Retrieved June 16, 2011, from http://www.wallacefoundation.org/KnowledgeCenter/KnowledgeTopics/CurrentAreasofFocus/EducationLeadership/Pages/learning-from-leadership-investigating-the-links-to-improved-student-learning.aspx.

Washor, E., & Mojkowski, C. (2006). High schools as communities in communities. *New Educator, 2*(3), 247–57.

Watts, G., & Castle, S. (1993). The time dilemma in school restructuring. *Phi Delta Kappan, 75*(4), 306–11.

White, S., & McIntosh, J. (2007). Data delivers a wake-up call: Five year plan unites teachers into a collaborative culture. *Journal of Staff Development, 28*(2), 30–35.

Wiggins, G., & McTighe, J. (2004). *Understanding by design: Professional development workbook*. Alexandria, VA: Association for Supervision and Curriculum Development.

Wiles, J. (2009). *Leading curriculum development*. Thousand Oaks, CA: Corwin.

Wirt, F., & Kirst, M. (2005). *The political dynamics of American education, 3rd ed*. Richmond, CA: McCutchan.

Wolk, R. (2010). Education: The case for making it personal. *Educational Leadership, 67*(7), 16–21.

Wolk, S. (2008). Joy in school. *Educational Leadership, 66*(1), 8–14.

Zinn, L. (1996). Philosophy of education inventory. In M. Katzenmeyer & G. Moller, *Awakening the sleeping giant: Leadership development for teachers* (pp. 103–34). Thousand Oaks, CA: Corwin.

~

About the Author

Marilyn Tallerico is professor of education at Binghamton University, State University of New York, where she coordinates the Educational Leadership program. She teaches graduate courses in curriculum leadership, supervision and staff development, politics of education, administrative internship, and leadership in educational settings. Prior to serving Binghamton, she was a faculty member at Syracuse University's School of Education for 17 years. She is widely published in both professional and research journals, including the *Educational Administration Quarterly*. Her three earlier books were *Supporting and Sustaining Professional Development: A Principal's Guide* (2005), *Accessing the Superintendency: The Unwritten Rules* (2000), and *City Schools: Leading the Way* (1993), the latter coedited with Patrick B. Forsyth. A theme throughout her work is how leaders can promote equity and quality in schools and districts.

Prior to her university positions, Marilyn served for 12 years in PreK–12 public schools in Connecticut and Arizona. She has been a central office curriculum director, a coordinator of bilingual and English-as-a-Second-Language programs, and a high school Spanish teacher. She earned her Ph.D. in Educational Leadership and Policy Studies at Arizona State University, and her master's and undergraduate degrees at the University of Connecticut. In addition to her professional interests, she is an avid outdoors person, a happy kayaker, and a hopeful golfer.